PAPAL PRIMACY
IN THE THIRD
MILLENNIUM

Papal Primacy in the Third Millennium

Russell Shaw

Our Sunday Visitor Publishing Division
Our Sunday Visitor, Inc.
Huntington, Indiana 46750

ISBN: 0-87973-555-4
LCCCN: 00-133654

Cover design by Monica Haneline
Cover photo courtesy of The Cathedral Museum of Fort Wayne, Indiana
PRINTED IN THE UNITED STATES OF AMERICA

Acknowledgments

I wish to express my appreciation to Dr. Germain Grisez for his numerous practical comments and suggestions regarding the first draft of this book.

The translation of Scripture used here is the *Revised Standard Version, Catholic Edition*. The translation of the documents of the Second Vatican Council is *Vatican Council II: The Conciliar and Post Conciliar Documents*, Austin Flannery, O.P., General Editor (Collegeville, Minn.: Liturgical Press, 1984). Quotations from Dante are from *The Divine Comedy of Dante Alighieri*, Allen Mandelbaum, trans. (New York: Bantam Books, 1982).

Contents

Introduction

Most adult Catholics are aware of the conflicts in Church life that followed the Second Vatican Council and continue in some respects today. While acknowledging recent tensions, Russell Shaw makes clear in this superb overview of the papacy that conflict has never been very far from Peter and his successors. And even though the last century has witnessed drastic changes in nearly every aspect of society and individual life, these same years have been a remarkably fruitful time for papal ministry.

Shaw tracks this renewal of the papal office to the ecumenical councils Vatican I and Vatican II. Because of their clear teaching on papal primacy and apostolic collegiality, these councils enabled the Church to overcome the problems that stemmed from centuries-long confusion about papal authority. They thus contributed to the development of strong (and effective) modern popes.

Many – myself certainly included — see Pope John Paul II as a model of papal strength, selflessly and fraternally exercised. Nearly eighty and in difficult health, he demonstrated in his pilgrimage to Jordan and Israel a force of character and a witness for peace unmatched by any other presence on the world stage.

For more than two decades, John Paul II has inspired those of us who are bishops in our own witness of faith. He also has worked tirelessly to lead all Christians to the full communion desired by Christ. In his 1995 encyclical *Ut Unum Sint* ("That They May Be One") he took the bold step of proposing a "patient and fraternal dialogue" toward finding ways of exercising papal primacy that could lead to perfecting Christian communion without compromising the essential mission of the Petrine office.

Although important within the ecumenical context, this unprecedented invitation of the pope has drawn an even more eager response from Catholic groups intent on changing the papacy. It is these proposals and the whole situation of the pope and Church at the dawn of the third Christian millennium that Russell Shaw focuses on in *Papal Primacy in the Third Millennium*.

Shaw has a career-long record of faithful and distinguished writing about the Church. With engaging skill, he outlines the historical foundations of the current debate. A seasoned journalist, he analyzes the various reform proposals without polemics. He also offers some proposals of his own, gleaned from his many years of service. The result is an outstanding, balanced, and very readable primer that ought to be enjoyed by everyone interested in the future of the Church.

✠ CHARLES J. CHAPUT, O.F.M. CAP.

ARCHBISHOP OF DENVER

CHAPTER ONE

Who Wants
to Tame the Pope?

The Pope of the universal Church shall be elected
for a single ten-year term by Delegates selected by
the National Councils. . . . The Pope together with
the General Council and their agencies and committees bear (sic) the main responsibility for carrying out the policies set by the General Council.

Association for the Rights of Catholics in the Church
A Proposed Constitution for the Catholic Church

Where else begin a book about the papacy except at the
Vatican? Or, in this case, in a restaurant three blocks down the
street?

Everybody around the Vatican knows Roberto's. This
modest two-room eating establishment is one of Rome's countless neighborhood restaurants, offering solid fare, unpreten-
tious decor, and not unreasonable prices. Situated down the
Borgo Pio from the Sant'Anna gate, it's a good place to look
for cardinals, bureaucrats of the Roman Curia, and journalists,
sitting cheek by jowl over pasta and wine. The last time I was
there, I was digging into *spaghetti con vongole* when the archbishop who heads one of the curial offices — dicasteries, they
are called — came in with an Irish-born Church official from
Venezuela. Soon after, one of the pope's personal aides breezed
by with two priest friends from the United States. That's
Roberto's.

One evening in early October 1994, back in Rome after a year, I was midway through my *riso al sugo* when the Eminent Vaticanologist entered and, spying me, sat down at my table. "Do you know," he said, "I've never had a meal here by myself!" A heavyset bald man with thick glasses, he wore a khaki shirt open at the throat, khaki trousers of a lighter shade, and a wrinkled gray jacket that he hung on a coat rack next to the table.

We had known each other for years and, though not exactly what you'd call friends, had retained the knack of speaking frankly to each other even while taking opposite sides on most Church issues. After a few pleasantries, he began talking shop.

"I heard on Vatican Radio that the European Parliament has a resolution criticizing the pope for his stand at the UN population conference in Cairo." (The Vaticanologist paused to help himself to a glass of wine from my quarter-liter carafe. "It's more Christian this way," he explained.) "I wonder if that's why he called off his trip to the United Nations — he was afraid of being censured? In that case the story about his leg needing time to heal [Pope John Paul had broken a bone in a fall several weeks earlier] was a cover — an excuse to stay home." He told the waiter to bring him *spaghetti carbonara* and a half-liter carafe of the house white.

"That seems improbable — about the UN, I mean," I said. "It's always gone out of its way to cultivate Vatican support. But I can certainly believe the secular establishment is furious with John Paul over what happened in Cairo. He got just about everything he wanted on abortion and quite a bit else. It's a sign of his success that they're so angry. If he hadn't been successful, they'd treat him as they usually treat religious figures — patronize him, I mean."

"No doubt." The Vaticanologist did not seem impressed.

"In any case, this pontificate is now in its final phase. John Paul will die, and then it will be, 'The Pope is dead, long live the Pope!' Nothing he's done will outlast him. Not the *Catechism*. Not *Veritatis Splendor*. Certainly not the document on the ordination of women.

"Why do you think he published that?" he added. "There's no really significant movement for the ordination of women in the Catholic Church today. He did it to tie the hands of his successor. But that won't work. The new man will put aside everything John Paul has done and start over. . . . I'm sorry to tell you that I cut up my spaghetti. Don't watch if it bothers you."

After a while I asked the waiter to bring me *sogliola griglia*. My companion ordered *lombatina di vitello*. And another half-liter of white. Becoming mellow, he said, "After all, this pontificate has been *very* Polish. Like a cavalry charge against tanks — an attempt at a Catholic restoration in the face of progressive secularization. It can't last."

I poured myself a glass of wine from his carafe to replace the one he'd taken from mine. Conversation meandered on. I said, "But don't you think it's the job of a pope to speak for the tradition — to identify a certain norm, a standard, for being Catholic?"

He scowled. "Membership in the Church is entirely voluntary, a matter of choice. This man tries to coerce people. Nobody appreciates that."

"I can think of many people who are great supporters of John Paul."

"Name three," he spat out, sawing vigorously at his cutlet. "The cardinals are going to want a change, and they'll choose a pope who will give them one. You say, 'What about all those bishops John Paul named?' Forget about them. They'll be with the new man, whoever he is."

Over *espresso*, accompanied by a large *Sambuca*, the Vaticanologist began to utter warnings. "After this pope is dead, Opus Dei and the 'movements,' as they're called — Communion and Liberation, the Neo-Catechumenate, and the rest — had better watch out. As Machiavelli said, it's a dangerous thing to be the favorite of the Prince. And I suppose you'll agree — the movements *have* been favorites in this pontificate? They're in for a good kicking-around when John Paul is gone. I tell you all this because I imagine you don't hear the truth very often."

He said some other things after that, but I forget what.

What 'Taming' Does and Doesn't Mean

It would be stretching the truth to say this book began that evening in Roberto's — stretching it, but not too far. The Vaticanologist's words made me more aware than I had been of a recognizable party in the Church composed of people who see things very much as he did. The Vaticanologist did not spell out their agenda that evening, but others have. A lot of it, I've come to see, involves "taming the pope."

Taming would mean removing authority from the papacy through a systematic program of decentralization, and vesting it in various other places — the Synod of Bishops, national bishops' conferences, local or "particular" churches (that is, dioceses), perhaps even other structures that don't yet exist. The watchwords of this decentralizing program are collegiality, subsidiarity, inculturation, pluralism, and — sometimes — democracy.

Structural change would be just the start. Going beyond a revolution in Church structures, the program looks to a revolution in Church teaching and discipline, and especially in the way Catholics think about the Church. A retired religion professor and canon lawyer, proprietor of a question-and-answer column on the website of a progressive Catholic group, told one inquirer, "Your question recalls the oft-repeated assertion that 'the church is not a democracy.' One contemporary reply to that is, 'Maybe not, but it ought to be.' "

Still, someone undertaking to write a book about taming the pope has to recognize a fundamental fact: By no means can all proposals for changes in the exercise of papal primacy be dismissed as radical or irresponsible. Some are, but not all. Moreover, the discussion of this question is necessary. Theological and historical questions need examining. Important practical purposes could be served by prudent modifications in how primacy is exercised. Responsible suggestions for doing so must be distinguished from attempts to weaken the papacy. That is not always easy to do.

How popes exercise their supreme authority to govern the Church has changed in the past, is changing now, and will go on changing in the future. A fossilized papacy would be a calamity. And recent popes — starting at least with Pius XII and continuing through John Paul II — have been notable innovators in this matter.

Pope John Paul specifically invited the discussion of primacy and its exercise in an encyclical on Christian unity called *Ut Unum Sint*, published in 1995. Its large-minded, generous-spirited approach makes it a remarkable document.

In this ecumenical age, John Paul writes, the mission of the Bishop of Rome is particularly directed to achieving "full unity" among Christians. For Catholics, reunion with the Eastern Churches has particular priority. In the search for unity — "the communion of the one Church willed by Christ" — it's important not to impose "any burden beyond that which is strictly necessary." Accompanying is a citation to chapter fifteen of the Acts of the Apostles, which tells of the decision reached by the apostles and elders of the Church in Jerusalem on what to require — and not require — of Gentile converts.

Turning to his own office, John Paul describes it in the time-honored phrase *servus servorum dei* — "servant of the servants of God." This title, he says, is "the best possible safeguard against the risk of separating power (and in particular the primacy) from ministry." But even though the ministry of the Bishop of Rome is "the visible sign and guarantor of unity," nevertheless it is an unhappy fact that the papal office is "a difficulty for most other Christians."

All the same, it is a hopeful sign that papal primacy has become a subject for study in ecumenical circles: "The other Churches and Ecclesial Communities are more and more taking a fresh look at this ministry of unity." Desiring to contribute to this process, John Paul then extends a remarkable invitation:

> As Bishop of Rome I am fully aware . . . that Christ ardently desires the full and visible communion of all those Communities in which . . . his Spirit dwells. I am convinced that I have a particular responsibility in this regard, above all in acknowledging the ecumenical aspirations of the majority of the Christian communities and in heeding the request made of me to find a way of exercising the primacy which, while in no way renouncing what is essential to its mission, is nonetheless open to a new situation. . . .
>
> This is an immense task, which we cannot refuse and which I cannot carry out by myself. Could not the real but imperfect communion existing between us persuade Church leaders and their theologians to engage with me in a patient and fraternal dialogue on this subject, a dialogue in which, leaving useless controversies behind, we could listen to one another, keeping before us only the will of Christ for his Church?

It is hard to imagine any pope before John Paul saying this and harder to imagine any after him not saying as much.

An Archbishop at Oxford

Probably the most widely publicized Roman Catholic response to *Ut Unum Sint* up to now was that of Archbishop John R. Quinn, retired archbishop of San Francisco, in a paper called "The Claims of the Primacy and the Costly Call to Unity," which was delivered on June 29, 1996, at the Jesuits' house at Oxford University, Campion Hall. Apparently as a result of advance priming of the press, it received international media coverage and stirred a discussion that still continues. He followed up in 1999 with a book (*The Reform of the Papacy: The Costly Call to Christian Unity*) developing some of his points — though on others the Oxford paper is clearer and more specific.

What he actually said at Oxford may not have mattered as much as the fact that he said it. Archbishop Quinn is a former president (1977-1980) of the National Conference of Catholic Bishops and the United States Catholic Conference, and widely considered to be one of the more intellectual American bishops. It was not unprecedented, but it was unusual, that so senior a figure in the hierarchy should speak out on papal primacy and related matters in terms which, though generally respectful, plainly were critical.

At a session held to discuss his Oxford paper during the American Academy of Religion's annual convention in November, 1997, a speaker deplored the fact that he'd had to "wait until after his retirement" to speak his mind. "The fact is, I did not wait," he replied. *Ut Unum Sint* appeared in May, 1995; he resigned as archbishop of San Francisco in December. Having been invited to speak at Oxford the following June, he was mulling a topic when a theologian friend suggested papal primacy. "It had not been in my mind prior to this," he explained.

So, what did he say?

Regarding the invitation in *Ut Unum Sint*: "The Pope has asked us for an honest and serious critique. He has every right to expect that this call will be heard and that this response will be especially forthcoming from those who recognize and reverence the primacy of the Roman Pontiff."

Regarding the "new situation" to which the encyclical referred: "The 'new situation' for the primacy is indeed comparable to the situation which confronted the primitive Church when it abandoned the requirements of the Mosaic Law and embraced the mission to the gentiles. . . . Similarly today, there are strong divisions within the Church and accompanying pressures pulling it in conflicting directions. The decisions required by the 'new situation' will be exacting and costly."

Regarding the collegiality of bishops: " 'Collegiality' is predicated of the Bishops precisely because with the Pope they have from Christ a true responsibility for the whole Church. . . . Collegiality does not exist in its fullest sense if the Bishops are merely passive recipients of papal directives and initiatives. Bishops are not only 'sub Petro' [under Peter]. They are also 'cum Petro' [with Peter]."

Archbishop Quinn then proceeded to his critique. A lot of it concerned reforming the Roman Curia — the Vatican agencies that collaborate with the pope in the central administration of the Church.

"It is self-evident that the Pope could not fulfill his responsibilities of communion and communication with more than three thousand bishops and dioceses in a wide diversity of cultures and languages without the Curia," he said. Furthermore, the Curia includes many men and women of "great intelligence, broad experience, great vision and exemplary holiness." But others are "very narrow, with limited experience, especially pastoral experience."

The Curia's way of doing things — a tendency to micro-manage is sometimes alleged — is an obstacle to other Christians who might be contemplating reunion with Rome, the archbishop said. But it's also a problem for some Catholic bishops. When the Curia exaggerates its role in the scheme of things, then "in place of the dogmatic structure comprised of the Pope and the rest of the Episcopate, there emerges a new and three-fold structure: the Pope, the Curia and the Episcopate." Then the Curia may try to exercise "oversight and authority" over bishops; papal nuncios sometimes are similarly tempted.

Against this background, he urged a "major structural reform" of the Curia by a commission of three — a representative of a bishops' conference, a representative of the Curia, and an unspecified layperson. Its recommendations would be presented for a vote to the presidents of bishops' conferences at a special meeting and only then turned over to the pope.

Without making it clear who he thought was to blame — pope, Curia, or both — the archbishop spoke of "concern all over the world" about recent decisions of the Holy See, both what was decided and how. The matters were said to include "the appointment of bishops, the approval of documents such as the *Catechism of the Catholic Church*, the grave decline in the numbers of priests and the consequent decline in the availability of Mass for the people, the cognate issue of celibacy of the clergy, the role of episcopal conferences, the role of women and the issue of the ordination of women."

The great need of the present moment, he maintained, is to put flesh on the bones of collegiality by working out the relationship between pope and bishops. Citing John Henry Newman's objection to the nineteenth-century definition of the dogma of papal infallibility (Newman accepted it as true but thought it inopportune to define it), he remarked: "While great emphasis has been given to the doctrinal aspects of the exer-

19

cise of the primacy, too little attention has been given to the place of prudence. . . . The doctrinal questions do not exhaust the discussion of primacy. There is a legitimate and necessary place for discussion of what is prudent at a given time in history."

So, for instance, before the pope issues doctrinal declarations or binding decisions in disciplinary and liturgical matters, bishops should be "seriously consulted" both individually and collectively in their national conferences. This would enable them to be "a better support to the Pope," while their visible participation in decisions would help win popular acceptance for what was decided.

The world Synod of Bishops should be strengthened. Bishops should be allowed to discuss what they want and make whatever recommendations to the pope they choose, instead of being pressured to avoid certain topics — those mentioned above and others, such as "divorce, remarriage and the reception of the Sacraments." ("I am not here taking a personal position on any of these issues," insisted Archbishop Quinn, who, as a delegate to the Synod of 1980, caused a furor by calling for a new look at the teaching on contraception.) The Synod ought to have a "deliberative vote" — it should be able to make definite proposals for the pope to accept or reject, not limited, as now, only to giving advice.

Similarly, there should be a fresh look at ecumenical councils. "The Council of Constance in the fifteenth century decreed that there should be regularly scheduled Councils every ten years. If that decree had been observed perhaps the history of the Reformation would have been different."

Other suggestions followed under the headings "Collegiality and the Sanctifying Office" and "Collegiality and the Office of Governing": bishops should be permitted to wrestle on their own with the issue of general absolution; the principle of "inculturation" should be applied more freely to the liturgy; the way bishops are chosen should be changed to provide "a meaningful and responsible role for priests, lay persons and religious."

In a key passage, Archbishop Quinn argued that the principle of subsidiarity should be accepted as applying to the Church. (People who hold this view consider subsidiarity the necessary underpinning of collegiality, decentralization, and the autonomy of the local churches.) Subsidiarity, an element of Catholic social doctrine, holds that what can be done at a lower level in a social system shouldn't be done at a higher one. Church documents often have commended subsidiarity as an important principle for organizing secular affairs; but whether and how it pertains to the Church are disputed.

In conclusion, the archbishop spoke of a tension between two "models" at work in the Church: the political and the ecclesial. "The fundamental concern of the political model is order and therefore control. The fundamental concern of the ecclesial model is communion and therefore discernment in faith of the diversity of gifts and works of the Spirit. . . . The ultimate question which the Pope — and all of us who seek the unity of Christians — must ask first and last is: 'What is the will of God?' "

Archbishop Quinn's Oxford paper was a clear statement of what might be called the moderate progressive position in the primacy debate. Anyone following this discussion soon becomes familiar with the program it espouses. Other views extend across the ideological spectrum from left to right. Not all are moderate, by any means.

An Old Argument

The primacy debate didn't begin in 1995 or 1996. In fact, the roots of many of today's "new" ideas about the papacy go back centuries; we shall trace a number of them in this book. In modern times, the debate is largely a legacy of the Second Vatican Council (1962-1965), which raised a number of important questions about ecclesiology — the theological study of the nature and structure of the Church — without answering them. The result has been a great deal of debate and advocacy.

As an example, consider a book called *The Remaking of the Church*, published in 1973 by Richard P. McBrien, then a theologian at Boston College and later at the University of Notre Dame. Here Father McBrien offered an analysis of the Church's situation and a prescription for its future very much like the program of progressive Catholicism today.

Clearly, he felt that the promise of Vatican Council II hadn't been realized. "What happened to the Catholic Church after the council?" he demanded. "Why did so many of its bright promises suddenly dim and go out? What precipitated the apparent decline and fall of the Catholic reform movement? What forces reduced that Church to the condition of 'bare ruined choirs'?" These remain good questions. Traditional Catholics answer them very differently from liberals, of course.

Father McBrien went on to lay out his program in an "Agenda for Reform." Here are many of the proposals still dear to the hearts of progressives: replace "monarchical absolutism" in Church governance with "some form of constitutionalism"; recognize the principle of subsidiarity in Church affairs; make national pastoral councils — such as the Dutch Pastoral Council — the policy-making bodies for the Church at the national and local levels; return to "the ancient and long-standing practice of the election of bishops by the clergy and laity"; and much else.

Comments under the heading "Papal Power" are particularly interesting.

[T]he Church must willingly, and perhaps painfully, demythologize its understanding of the papacy. . . . While [the pope] remains the symbol of faith and unity for all the churches of the world, and while his office retains, in principle, the greatest authority for moral and doctrinal utterance, the Pope himself can no longer function as an absolute monarch. . . .

General policy decisions affecting the universal Church should be reserved, not to the Pope alone, but to the Pope and the International Synod of Bishops. The function of the Curia is to assist in the execution of these decisions . . . . Problems which are national, not international, in character should be within the competence of the national conference of bishops rather than the Pope, and the same would be true of problems at regional and diocesan levels, in keeping with the Church's fundamental principle of subsidiarity. The election of the Pope by the International Synod of Bishops rather than by the College of Cardinals and some limitation of tenure (e.g., ten years, renewable) would serve to modify the present absolutely monarchical pattern.

That was 1973. It could be written today, and might be written tomorrow. The ideas are central to taming the pope.

Recent Developments

Yet *Ut Unum Sint* really did introduce something new into the primacy debate. Especially, it lent the weight of papal authority to the discussion of changes for the sake of ecumenism and collegiality. The encyclical thereby legitimated the debate and raised it to a new level of seriousness. Now someone with an idea she or he wants to float can point to an invitation from the Pope. And although the invitation hardly bestows *a priori* papal approval on any and every suggestion, it has opened the doors more widely than in a long time to consideration of these matters.

One instance of serious reflection was a theological symposium in Rome in December, 1996, organized by the Vatican's Congregation for the Doctrine of the Faith, that brought together scholars from Europe and North America. The proceedings have been published by the Vatican press under the title *Il Primato del Successore di Pietro* ("The Primacy of the Successor of Peter"). I shall refer frequently to papers presented there.

Another instance, of an ecumenical kind, is "The Gift of Authority," an "agreed statement" published in May, 1999, by the Second Anglican-Roman Catholic International Commission, the official international Anglican-Catholic dialogue body known as ARCIC-II. Its members and staff include two dozen Anglican and Roman Catholic bishops and scholars from Great Britain, the United States, Canada, and several other countries. The cochairmen were the Rt. Rev. Mark Santer, Anglican bishop of Birmingham, England, and the Most Rev. Cormac Murphy-O'Connor, bishop of Arundel and Brighton at the time the statement was published and later named by John Paul II archbishop of Westminster. "The Gift of Authority" follows and builds on a 1976 ARCIC statement that declared in part: "It seems appropriate that in any future union a universal primacy . . . should be held by that See [Rome]."

To judge from the reception it has received, whether "The Gift of Authority" is a sign of hope, pie in the sky, or theological flimflam depends on the reader's point of view and preexisting biases. It has been called all those things and, at the time this is written, seems to be particularly controversial in Anglican circles. Personally, I take it as a sign of hope, although one that raises a number of obvious questions and difficulties. We need to look at it here not because it marks a definitive break-through — pretty clearly, it doesn't — but for the light it sheds on the primacy debate.

Among the reasons for taking encouragement cited by "The Gift of Authority" is the invitation in *Ut Unum Sint* to "fraternal dialogue on how the particular ministry of unity of the Bishop of Rome might be exercised in a new situation." ARCIC-II's answer is complex and not without ambiguity. It seems to boil down to this: Provided papal authority to teach and govern the Church were sufficiently hemmed in by the principle of collegiality and by appropriate accompanying structures of a "synodical" sort, Anglicans — at least Anglicans of the kind connected with ARCIC-II — could find it acceptable. In fact, the statement goes on to say:

> The Commission's work has resulted in sufficient agreement on universal primacy as a gift to be shared, for us to propose that such a primacy could be offered and received even before our churches are in full communion. Both Roman Catholics and Anglicans look to this ministry being exercised in collegiality and synodality — a ministry of *servus servorum Dei*. We envisage a primacy that will even now help to uphold the legitimate diversity of traditions, strengthening and safeguarding them in fidelity to the Gospel.

"The Gift of Authority" goes so far as to suggest that Anglican bishops accompany Roman Catholic bishops on the *ad limina* visits the latter make to Rome every five years to confer with the pope and testify to communion with him. Whatever else anyone might think of all this, it surely is far removed from the days of Henry VIII and Elizabeth I, St. Thomas More and St. John Fisher, Archbishop Cranmer and Archbishop Laud.

But the negative reactions to "The Gift of Authority" also deserve to be noted.

Some Roman Catholics are unpersuaded that the version of primacy sketched by ARCIC-II would be either workable in practice or acceptable from a doctrinal point of view. They suspect the Anglican signers have no more than a primacy of honor in mind; and they fear that a papacy structured along the lines suggested would be too hobbled in its ability to teach and govern the Church.

Collegiality, in this context, might be taken to mean the pope could only act in company with the college of bishops, never on his own. Requiring that he function within "synodical" structures might imply an extreme version of the theological notion of "reception": unless people agreed, what the pope said would carry no weight. And although collegiality and reception are valid ideas up to a point, such people conclude, beyond that point they contradict the supreme, universal, immediate, and unimpeded primacy of the pope and his authority to govern the Church as he deems necessary, as these matters of dogma were defined by the First Vatican Council and reaffirmed by Vatican Council II.

Some other Roman Catholics objected to "The Gift of Authority" on quite different grounds. Soon after its publication, Hans Küng, the Swiss theologian whose disapproval of Pope John Paul II and the Curia is well known, ripped into it as an Anglican sell-out that "strengthens the unrepentant representatives of a medieval Counter-Reformation Roman system and rejects the advocates of the renewal of the Catholic Church."

Then, does it really help to suggest that the papal primacy might commend itself to the Anglican Communion because patterns of primacy exist in both Churches?

It is precisely in those patterns that the difference lies. A primate who is *primus inter pares* [first among equals], as recognised by the Anglican Communion (and by the Orthodox in the case of the Ecumenical Patriarch [of Constantinople]) is very far from a primate who exercises a centralising and absolutist domination on the Roman pattern. Would it not do enormous damage to ecumenism if this Anglican charism were to be lost in a thrust towards centralisation?

Anglican voices have been heard to the same effect.

A different sort of critique comes from Father Geoffrey Kirk, secretary of an Anglican group called Forward in Faith, which opposes the Church of England's 1992 decision to ordain women as priests. Pronouncing ARCIC-II's position on authority "wholly incredible," he likens it to the "confusion and obfuscation" said to be presently practiced by the Anglican Church to maintain a facade of communion between those who accept women's ordination and those who reject it.

It's been clear for a long time that, given proper circumstances and guarantees, some Anglicans — perhaps some Orthodox, too — might accept a papal primacy of honor: *primus inter pares*, as Hans Küng puts it. (In fairness, "The Gift of Authority" can reasonably be read as suggesting something more than that.) Indeed, back in 1920, Adrian Fortescue could confidently say of the "Romanising section" of the Church of England: "The Anglican of this school could submit to a constitutional papacy, not to the arbitrary rule now claimed by the Pope." But is a "constitutional papacy" or a primacy of honor an adequate expression of the supreme authority of the pope? Evidently not, if the teaching of Vatican I and Vatican II is taken seriously.

Pending further clarification, this upbeat but ambiguous

episode in recent Anglican-Roman Catholic relations illustrates the truth of a remark by Cardinal Joseph Ratzinger, prefect of the Congregation for the Doctrine of the Faith under John Paul II. Although it would be unrealistic to look for "a general re-union of Christendom based on the papacy in the foreseeable future," he once said, nevertheless the papacy already serves a unity transcending the communion of the Roman Catholic Church: "Even when the claims of his office are disputed the pope remains a point of personal reference in the world's sight for the responsibility he bears and expresses for the word of faith. . . . In this sense even in division the papacy has a function of establishing unity." Too hopeful? Christianity is a hopeful religion.

A Constitution for the Church

One other document deserves our attention at this point — the proposed Constitution for the Catholic Church from which the passage quoted at the start of this chapter comes.

The Catholic Church always has had a constitution, in the sense that certain doctrines and principles determine its essential structure and manner of operating. This basic constitution was given by Christ and cannot be altered. Although the Church does not possess a written constitution like the "Constitution for the Catholic Church," the practical equivalent exists in documents of its Magisterium, or teaching authority, in particular Vatican Council I's "Dogmatic Constitution on the Church of Christ," *Pastor Aeternus* ("The Eternal Pastor"), Vatican Council II's "Dogmatic Constitution on the Church," *Lumen Gentium*, the 1983 Code of Canon Law for the Western Church, and the Code of Canons of Eastern Churches, in effect since 1991. (For much of the nearly quarter-century during which the 1983 Code was under development, serious thought was given to separately publishing a *Lex Ecclesiae*

28

Fundamentis — "Fundamental Law of the Church" — as a form of constitution. The idea eventually was rejected, but much of the draft of the proposed Fundamental Law was incorporated into the Code.)

The Constitution for the Catholic Church is a sharp departure from the vision of the Church as a hierarchically structured communion as it is contained in the sources just mentioned. It sees authority in the Church flowing from the bottom up, in the manner of a secular representative democracy or a "people's church" of the kind advocated by liberation theologians like the Brazilian Leonardo Boff.

Described as "intended for the governance of the whole Catholic Church," this document is the joint product of an American group called the Association for the Rights of Catholics in the Church and some European progressives. It was presented as a working document at a conference of the European Network of Rights in the Church held in January, 1999, and has been taken up by an umbrella group called the International Movement We Are Church. An Internet notice inviting comments and responses promises a revised version in 2001.

The constitution enunciates a number of principles supported by Catholics of the left. For example: "All Catholics have the right and responsibility to follow their informed consciences in all matters"; in the Church there is a "legitimacy of responsible dissent and pluralism and its expression"; "all Catholics have the right to withdraw from a marriage which has irretrievably broken down (and) retain the radical right to remarry"; all Catholics have a right "to receive all the sacraments for which they are adequately prepared (and) to exercise all ministries in the Church for which they are adequately prepared"; and, lest anyone miss the point of that, "all Catholic women have an equal right with men to the resources and the exercise of all the powers of the Church."

Regarding Church governance, the constitution declares its unreserved commitment to subsidiarity, as well as to the principle that people in leadership positions should be elected for specified terms. "Representative councils" made up of elected members are the "principal decision-making bodies" at every level, international, national, diocesan, and local. For the universal Church, the constitution envisages a system whereby, every ten years, the national councils would elect a five-hundred-member General Council responsible for "policies and regulations concerning doctrine, morals, worship, education, social outreach, administration, finances and other activities carried out in the name of the universal Church, bearing especially in mind the principle of subsidiarity." Its cochairpersons would be the pope and a layperson elected by the council.

And what of the pope? The General Council is responsible for choosing him or her, although here the constitution grows unaccountably vague. On the one hand, the council is to establish a papal election commission, but its duties are not spelled out. On the other hand: "The Pope of the universal Church shall be elected for a single ten-year term by Delegates selected by the National Councils." The number of delegates from each country shall be proportional to the number of registered Catholics. The election is to take place at a Papal Election Congress.

Thereafter: "The Pope together with the General Council and their agencies and committees bear the main responsibility for carrying out the policies set by the General Council, especially in the areas of worship, doctrinal, moral and spiritual instruction, and pastoral care functions of the universal Church, bearing in mind the principle of subsidiarity." Allegations of "illegal or unconstitutional actions by the Pope" shall be heard by a Supreme Tribunal established by the General

Council. Whether she or he should be removed from office is for the council to decide.

The sponsors of the Constitution for the Catholic Church don't expect their document to be adopted anytime soon. Their aim is to get its ideas on the table and move the debate in their direction. No doubt the constitution is a radical document. Yet many of its principles, and structures and processes similar to those it recommends, already are familiar themes in the primacy debate.

In an introduction to the draft, Leonard Swidler, a Temple University religion professor who heads the Association for the Rights of Catholics in the Church, says that for a constitution like this to become reality, "a change in the consciousness or mentality" of Catholics must occur. Since the experience of living in the Church needs to be understood as a "sharing in democracy," the constitution's sponsors urge continued reflection on "democratic Catholicism."

"The journey to a written and adopted 'Constitution for the Catholic Church' will doubtless be long, arduous and probably also serpentine. But it is a journey that a growing number of Catholics increasingly feel must be undertaken," Professor Swidler writes.

Taming the pope is both a necessary condition for this trip and its destination.

About This Book

I am not a theologian or historian, and this book isn't a work of theology or history, even though it has elements of both. Its basic purpose is to explain the discussion of papal primacy and clarify the issues for the benefit of people who may not be familiar with them. It is an exercise in the journalism of ideas.

Readers are entitled to know my personal biases — not

that these are important in themselves but because they color what I say. I favor a strong papacy and a reasonably high degree of central authority in the Church, believing this represents Christ's will and is in the best interests of ecclesial communion. I also favor episcopal collegiality and strong diocesan bishops. Perhaps naïvely, I do not see a necessary conflict between a strong pope and strong bishops. As a matter of fact, tension and conflict are more likely when one side or the other in this relationship is weaker than it should be.

Plainly, there are quite a few unresolved questions about the connection between primacy and collegiality. The current discussion of these matters should be welcomed. As for national conferences of bishops, I view them as necessary, desirable structures in today's Church, even though, for reasons that will become clear below, I am leery of proposals to give them more power than they already have.

I do not doubt that responsible, well thought-out changes in the exercise of papal primacy and in other processes and structures of the Church are needed. If the papal office and the rest of the Church ever stop changing, that will be because they have died; and although, as a matter of faith, I do not believe that can happen, its practical equivalent could. It would consist in the Church's being so frozen into old ideas and old ways of doing things that the changes needed for revitalization — in response to "a new situation," as Pope John Paul says — could not take place.

At this moment in history, no one's view of the papacy can help but be deeply influenced by his or her view of John Paul II. His admirers — I am one — naturally tend to favor the exercise of papal authority as he has exercised it. Those who view him with disfavor — the Eminent Vaticanologist is an example — naturally tend the other way. When the Australian theologian Paul Collins writes, "The Wojtyla papacy is the most powerful in history," he isn't misstating history in order to praise John Paul.

Given other times and other popes, the shoe might be on the other foot — progressives like the Vaticanologist and Father Collins might desire a strong, centralized papacy, while traditionalists would favor decentralization. Setting aside as much as possible opinions about the present pope and his policies, it is necessary to ask: What is the *right* alignment of relationships in the Church? More simply, as Archbishop Quinn puts it, "What is the will of God?"

In seeking answers, we need to realize that not everything that might be theologically or theoretically possible is also desirable. Our analysis has to operate on two levels: what *could* be done and what *should*? Even if theology raises no objections, what good sense rules out shouldn't be tried.

The emphasis here is on the pope's primacy of jurisdiction — his authority to govern the Church and the service (Petrine ministry) thus rendered — not on papal infallibility as such. People sometimes speak of "primacy of jurisdiction" on the one hand and "primacy of teaching" (infallibility) on the other, but that can get confusing. Here "primacy" means jurisdiction and only that.

Primacy and infallibility are linked, but they are not the same. As an everyday matter, primacy is by far the more important of the two — "far more crucial to the life of the Church," as the theologian Michael Buckley, S.J., remarks. This is not to dismiss infallibility as unimportant; but scholars say the charism of papal infallibility — the pope's divinely guaranteed power to "define" a dogma of faith without the possibility of falling into error in regard to what is defined — may formally have come into play only a dozen or so times in two thousand years; whereas the supreme authority of the Vicar of Christ to govern the universal Church is exercised daily as he establishes dioceses, appoints and transfers bishops, legislates, and otherwise does what popes routinely do.

This book is not apologetics. If it were, I would spend a lot of time "proving" papal primacy by examining texts like Matthew 16:13-19 (". . . you are Peter, and on this rock I will build my church . . .") or the Letter of Clement, an early Christian document (written around the year 95) that takes it for granted the Church at Rome can lay down the law to another church. In the early years, the Petrine succession — not just one Bishop of Rome succeeding another, but each understanding that he succeeds to the office and authority first held by Peter — takes place, in Henri de Lubac's words, "quietly, by simply taking place, without theoretical expositions, claims or an arsenal of proofs — and that is what could rightly be expected."

But rather than argue the case for papal primacy, I merely take my stand with what Newman says about the testimony of the early Church to its reality. In *An Essay on the Development of Christian Doctrine*, the book he wrote while wrestling throughout 1845 with whether to become a Roman Catholic, he speaks of "a partial fulfillment, or at least indications of what was to be," in those very early times. "Faint one by one, at least they are various, and are found in writers of many times and countries, and thereby illustrative of one another, and forming a body of proof." Several pages of citations from the Fathers and Church councils Newman knew and loved so well next follow. Then, rather abruptly, this: "More ample testimony of the Papal supremacy, as now professed by Roman Catholics, is scarcely necessary."

Having finished the *Essay on Development*, Newman — as people said in those days — went over to Rome.

CHAPTER TWO

Papal Primacy in History

"Take the place," said Constantine to Pope Sylvester. "It's all yours. . . . Rome is heathen and always will be. Yes, I know, you've got the tombs of Peter and Paul. I hope I have not shown myself insensible to that distinction. But why are they here? Simply because the Romans murdered them. That's the plain truth. Why, they even thought of murdering *me*. It's an ungodly place, your holiness, and you're welcome to it. One must start something *new*. I've got the site, very central; it will make a sublime port. The plans are drawn. Work will start at once on a great *Christian* capital, in the very centre of Christendom."

Evelyn Waugh
Helena

Looked at it from the Church's point of view, it's not entirely clear whether Constantine was a blessing or a curse. Possibly a bit of both. Naturally it was a relief to have the threat of bloody persecution removed, but the smothering bear hug with which Constantine (c. 285-337) embraced Christianity is another matter. For he was emperor, and everyone knew that Roman emperors were supreme in religious affairs as well as affairs of state.

In fact, people then hardly distinguished the two: the

empire, after all, was *one*, and emperors were the glue that held it together in all its parts. Even though Constantine acknowledged the unique sacramental powers of the Christian priests, he took it for granted that, where everything else of importance was concerned, he was master of the Church. This casual Caesaropapism defined attitudes and set patterns of behavior that would plague Christianity for a millennium and a half; even now they may not have entirely disappeared.

It is testimony to Constantine's deep and lasting influence that the anonymous author of a famous forgery called the Donation of Constantine, perhaps composed in the fifth century to strengthen the papacy against the Byzantine emperor (others put the date of composition between 750 and 850 and attribute it to a Frankish source), took it for granted that the central prerogatives of the papacy, while originating with God, at least had passed through the emperor's hands on their way to the pope. Constantine is supposed to have written:

> And we command and decree that he [the pope] should have primacy over the four principal Sees of Antioch, Alexandria, Constantinople and Jerusalem, as well as over all the Churches of God throughout the whole world; and the Pontiff who occupies at any given moment the See of that same most holy Roman Church shall rank as the highest and chief among all the priests of the whole world and by his decision all things are to be arranged concerning the worship of God or the security of the faith of Christians.

Hard to say whether God or Caesar is conferring authority on the pope, and the implications weren't lost on Dante. "Ah, Constantine," he exclaimed, "what wickedness was born — / and not from your conversion — from the dower / that you bestowed upon the first rich father!" A mixed blessing, to say the least.

What follows is not a "history" of papal primacy but only a sketch indicating some stages in the process by which the Church's understanding of primacy grew and deepened. As one might expect, this process was neither steady nor unimpeded; and it was precisely the assaults on papal authority that, in the long run, did the most to call forth the doctrine.

And, as suggested, Constantine had a lot to do with it.

The snatch of fanciful dialogue by Evelyn Waugh beginning this chapter recalls the emperor's fateful decision to transfer his capital to a new city, Constantinople, built on the shores of the Bosphorus at the place where Europe and Asia meet. Although Constantine thus unwittingly set the stage for East-West tensions for centuries to come, still the move was a boon for the papacy in significant respects. The Church in the East was tightly controlled by the emperors and accepted that condition, with patriarchs of Constantinople tending to play the role of court bishops; but geographical separation put psychic distance between the Bishop of Rome and the imperial court.

This independence was precarious, however, and often compromised. That is dramatically clear from the scandalous conflict between Emperor Justinian (483-565) and Pope Vigilius (pope from 537 to 555). Justinian was a remarkable man, one of the greatest who ruled from Constantinople. Today he is best remembered for having seen to the updating and codification of the empire's law, which served as the basis for much subsequent law, even up to the present, and for having rebuilt the famous church of Hagia Sophia; but in his time he took it for granted that he was to be involved in all religious affairs without exception.

Hoping to placate those among his subjects who believed that Christ had one nature, not two, Justinian sought the support of Pope Vigilius, a man of dubious character who already had been compromised by collusion in his predecessor's shameful removal from office at imperial behest. Arrested by Byzantine police while celebrating Mass in Rome, Vigilius was hauled off to Constantinople and there subjected to eight years of physical and psychological coercion, including house arrest, condemnation by a council convened by the emperor, threat of deposition, and the imprisonment of his advisers. Having at last given the emperor the form of words he sought, Vigilius was allowed to leave. He died of gallstones in Sicily. "The Emperor respected and honored the bishop of Rome," the Greek Orthodox author of a glowing biography of Justinian remarks.

Poor Vigilius's case was extreme but not unique. Historians speak of a "Byzantine captivity" of the papacy lasting centuries. Newly elected popes had to be confirmed by the emperor in Constantinople before being consecrated. Popes who resisted the imperial will suffered for it — for example, Pope St. Silverius, Bishop of Rome before Vigilius, who was deposed, exiled, and forced to abdicate the papal office, dying soon after of starvation and physical hardships.

Over the centuries, nevertheless, courageous popes struggled to be free. St. Leo the Great (pope from 440 to 461) strongly asserted papal authority and provided a theoretical exposition that was to stand for more than a thousand years. St. Gregory the Great (pope from 590 to 604) greatly advanced the temporal power of the popes and is considered founder of the medieval papacy.

The East-West Split

All this time the divisions between the Church of the West and the Churches of the East were growing. In *Ut Unum Sint* Pope John Paul speaks with appreciation of the first millennium as a time when Christianity in the West and in the East enjoyed undivided unity: "If today at the end of the second millennium we are seeking to restore full communion, it is to that unity, thus structured, which we must look." Wishing to emphasize the positive, he maintains discreet silence about some of the darker aspects of those first thousand years.

Unity was often strained and sometimes fractured. The definitive rupture in the year 1054, when pope and patriarch excommunicated each other, was not an isolated event but the final incident in a long, unhappy drama marked by misunderstanding, recurring tension, and sometimes outright conflict. Culture, politics, personalities, and power struggles all were part of it; clashing visions of the Church were at the theological root of the trouble. Of special importance in this process of drawing apart was the contribution of Photius, a gifted Patriarch of Constantinople who in the ninth century made a slashing theoretical argument against Rome's claim to primacy. In an encyclical letter written in 866 and directed to Eastern archbishops, Photius denounced various practices of the Western Church as heretical and castigated the "cruel tyranny" of the Bishop of Rome. In this light, the parting of the ways two centuries later looks predictable.

It is a disputed question today just how the Churches of the East did view the Church of Rome and its bishop during the first millennium. The question may grow more sensitive, and possibly more disputed, in the days ahead, as relationships between Rome and some Orthodox Churches improve.

Father Asterios Gerostergios, Justinian's biographer, denies that that emperor recognized the Bishop of Rome as anything more than first in honor among the patriarchs. "With regard to favorable comments made by Justinian to the Pope," he writes, "we can say that they were simple courtesies shown to him, without significance, because the authority of the Pope extended only to the Western Provinces. . . . For Justinian, the

Church of Rome was the Patriarchate of the West, and its Bishop just one of the five Patriarchs." An Orthodox theologian, Philip Sherrard, states:

> [T]he Roman conception of the Church on earth as a vast social and corporational organization whose supreme jurisdictional and magisterial powers are vested in the papacy cuts right across the patristic conception in which all such powers are vested in the episcopate as a whole and are exercised not only by each bishop acting independently in his own diocese but when necessary through the system of church councils. . . . [S]ince this Roman conception is incompatible and irreconcilable with that of the patristic tradition the attempt to implement it on the historical plane could not but produce a schism between those churches which accepted it and those which did not.

The underlying cause of the East-West schism, this author adds, was and is "the clash of these two fundamentally irreconcilable ecclesiologies." Similar sentiments now are sometimes expressed by Roman Catholics in the primacy debate.

More commonly, though, Catholic theologians and apologists take a very different view, citing patristic and conciliar sources in support of Roman and papal authority — for example, Newman in the *Development of Doctrine*. The present consensus view of primacy during the first millennium is summed up by Klaus Schatz, S.J. In his historical overview, *Papal Primacy*, he says that, at least in cases of conflict over matters of faith, "Rome was not said to be on the same level with the other patriarchs, but had a special role. . . . [But] the question of the ultimate center of Church unity was not posed in such well-defined terms because the East, unlike the West, subsisted on the basis of a union of Church and empire."

Let us leave this subject (for the moment) with the words of St. Basil the Great (329-379), one of the greatest of the Eastern Fathers. Imploring Pope Damasus to come to Cappadocia (in modern Turkey), where Basil served as bishop, in order to restore unity among its divided Christians, he wrote that the Arian heresy had reappeared in his region and was "producing its deadly fruit. . . . The champions of orthodoxy have been exiled from their churches by calumny and outrage, and the control of affairs has been handed over to men who are leading captive the souls of the simpler brethren." And what did he want of Pope Damasus? No less than the exercise of his primacy. "I have come to see the visit of your mercifulness as the only possible solution of our difficulties," St. Basil explained.

The Early Middle Ages

As the Middle Ages took shape, the stage gradually was set for a great expansion in the understanding and exercise of papal primacy. Indeed, so great would this expansion eventually be that the nineteenth-century Church historian Ignaz von Döllinger denounced it as "more artificial and sickly than sound and natural." (Note that the unhappy von Döllinger was excommunicated in 1871 by the archbishop of Munich for persistent and aggressive opposition to the definition of papal infallibility.)

Equally if not more significant than that influential forgery the Donation of Constantine, and the particular target of von Döllinger's wrath, was another, partial forgery known to history as the "False Decretals." Apparently composed around the year 850 in the diocese of Le Mans, France, this was a body of documents in Church law claiming to go as far back as the second century. As a matter of fact, a number of the docu-

41

ments were authentic; but others were the work of a skillful pseudonymous forger known to us as Isidore Mercator (Isidore the Merchant).

Doubts about authenticity surfaced as early as the Renaissance, but canonists continued to esteem the collection until well into the seventeenth century. "The real importance of the False Decretals is the new detail they bring in support of the already existing acceptance of the Roman Primacy," a historian says. They didn't invent the idea of primacy, but they seemed to provide detailed evidence of its functioning from a very early date.

It was not forged documents, however, but external pressure pointing in the opposite direction that more than anything spurred the development of the doctrine of primacy. The pressure came largely from emperors and kings, with the Church's full appreciation of papal authority forged in a titanic Church-State contest in the West beginning in the early Middle Ages and extending over the next half-millennium.

Charlemagne plays a crucial role in this story. By crowning Charlemagne emperor in a ceremony in Rome on Christmas Day in 800, Pope Leo III unintentionally created a rival power that for centuries to come would contest with the papacy for recognition as the supreme authority in Christendom. In some ways it was Constantine all over again, but with a difference: this emperor wasn't far off in Constantinople but uncomfortably close at hand.

Like his imperial predecessors, Charlemagne had no doubts about who was in charge of the Church. The pope and clergy had special sacral powers, but in other matters the emperor was number one. Accordingly, he did not hesitate to legislate minutely for ecclesiastical institutions and personnel. For example, "That no bishops, abbots, priests, deacons — no one, in short, belonging to the clergy — shall presume to have hunting dogs or hawks, falcons or sparrow-hawks." It was very likely a good idea, but not what most people now would consider the emperor's business.

For political, and even military, reasons, however, popes often had to look to temporal rulers for patronage and protection. The relationship already is clear in a letter Charlemagne sent Pope Leo in the year 796.

> It is our part with the help of Divine holiness to defend by armed strength the holy Church of Christ everywhere from the outward onslaught of the pagans and the ravages of the infidels, and to strengthen within it the knowledge of the Catholic Faith. It is your part, most holy Father, to help our armies with your hands lifted up to God like Moses, so that by your intercession and by the leadership and gift of God the Christian people may everywhere and always have the victory over the enemies of His Holy Name.

As an institution thoroughly inculturated in feudal society, the Church was constantly at risk of being co-opted and controlled by feudal structures of temporal governance. And frequently it succumbed.

From Canossa to Anagni

The biggest problem was lay investiture — kings and princes bestowing office on bishops and abbots, local lords choosing their parish priests, the secular power structure running the Church. Ending lay investiture was a particular aim of the program of ecclesial reform launched in the tenth century by the Benedictine monastery of Cluny in France. The struggle came to a head in the pontificate of Pope St. Gregory VII (1073-1085), who, as the monk Hildebrand, was for years a leading figure in the reform movement and served as adviser to several popes before becoming pope himself.

The story of Gregory's conflict with the German king Henry IV has been told and retold many times. The events of January, 1077, at Canossa, where the excommunicated king stood outside a castle in the snow for three days begging pardon from the pope, embedded themselves in Western memory. So much so, in fact, that Chancellor Bismarck, embroiled in a struggle with the Church in Germany in the late nineteenth century, had no need to explain what he meant in saying *he* wouldn't go to Canossa. Gregory's death in exile, the triumph of his policies in an agreement worked out forty-five years afterward by a later pope and emperor — these things are well known.

Just as important, if not more, was Pope Gregory's high doctrine of the papacy, set forth in a series of talking-points called *Dictatus Papae*. "Only the Roman bishop deserves to be called universal. . . . Only he can depose or absolve bishops. . . . Important cases from every church must be referred to him. He may not be judged by anyone. . . . He may depose emperors." Of these "extraordinary claims" historian Robert Louis Wilken writes: "He saw, as no one had before him, that the pope had to be more than a symbolic head of the Church. The Bishop of Rome was not simply the court of last appeal; the pope was called to *govern* the universal Church."

Historians generally agree that papal authority in the Middle Ages reached its high-water mark during the pontificate of Pope Innocent III, which extended from 1198 to 1216. Innocent's view of his office is reflected in the fact that he was the first consistently to refer to the pope as "Vicar of Christ." (Nearly eight centuries later the Second Vatican Council, in the Dogmatic Constitution on the Church, *Lumen Gentium*, would make the point that bishops, too, are "vicars and legates of Christ.") Earlier, the custom was to call the Bishop of Rome

"Vicar of Peter," but to Innocent III this fell short of what was demanded by the vision of a united Christendom under the headship of two great authorities, emperor and pope — and especially pope. He wrote:

> Just as God, founder of the universe, has constituted two large luminaries in the firmament of Heaven, a major one to dominate the day and a minor one to dominate the night, so he has established in the firmament of the Universal Church . . . two great dignities, a major one to preside, so to speak, over the days of the souls, and a minor one to preside over the nights of the bodies. They are the Pontifical authority and the royal power. . . . [T]he royal power derives from the Pontifical authority the splendor of its dignity.

The vision would become a nightmare at a place called Anagni.

The pontificate of Boniface VIII (pope from 1294 to 1303) is regarded as one of the most momentous in history. Like Pope St. Gregory VII's struggle with Henry IV, the story of Boniface's struggle with the French king Philip the Fair has been told and retold: how the two fell out over Philip's unauthorized taxation of the clergy; how the king maneuvered to bend the papacy to his policy and, that failing, mounted a propaganda campaign against the pope; how the imperious Boniface, having tried appeasement, turned truculent, declaring, "Our predecessors have three times deposed a king of France. Although we are not worth our predecessor's feet, we would turn out this king as though he were a footman."

The most remarkable papal response to the threat was the bull *Unam Sanctam* of November 18, 1302. Here what is called the "two swords" theory was pressed to its breaking point.

> We are taught by the words of the Gospel that in this Church and in its power there are two swords, a spiritual, to wit, and a temporal. . . . Wherefore both are in the power of the Church, namely the spiritual and material swords; the one, indeed, to be wielded by the Church, the other for the Church; the former by the priest, the latter by the hand of kings and knights, but at the will and sufferance of the priest. For it is necessary that one sword should be under another and that the temporal authority should be subjected to the spiritual.

Philip replied by organizing a virtual schism in France.

In September, 1303, Boniface was at his palace in Anagni readying a bull of excommunication against the king. Philip's agent William de Nogaret gathered a band of armed ruffians, soldiers of Boniface's bitter enemies the Colonna family, under the command of Sciarra Colonna. Storming the town on September 7, they burst into the papal palace. Historian Philip Hughes describes what happened next: "They found the old pope prepared for them, robed and clasping his crucifix. Nogaret demanded that he withdraw the excommunication and surrender himself for judgment. He replied that he would rather die. Sciarra Colonna offered to kill the pope. The cooler-headed Frenchman held him back. Then Colonna struck the old man in the face."

The outraged townspeople rose up against the invaders and forced them to flee. Boniface, a broken man by now, returned to Rome and died there on October 20. So shocking had the incident been that even Dante, who despised Boniface and in *The Divine Comedy* consigned him to hell, was moved to write (putting the words in the mouth of Hugh Capet, founder of the line of French kings to which Philip the Fair belonged):

I see the fleur-de-lis enter Anagni
and, in His vicar, Christ made prisoner.
I see him mocked a second time; I see
the vinegar and gall renewed — and He
is slain between two thieves now still alive.

The papacy had been deeply wounded and weakened. Whatever claims to supreme spiritual authority future popes might make, one of the two swords had been sheathed for good. It was the death knell for the vision of a united Christendom under Christ's Vicar. Soon, theorists like Marsilius of Padua were arguing that the state was superior to the Church and that, within the Church, a general council was superior to the pope.

The Rise of Conciliarism

Even so, popes did not abandon their claim to primacy. In fact, the disastrous "Babylonian captivity" (1309-1377), when the papal court was at Avignon and the French throne dominated the papacy, brought with it a marked centralization of administration and finances focusing on the pope and the Curia. Blessed Urban V (pope from 1362 to 1370) was the first pontiff to set out a clear claim to authority to name patriarchs, bishops, and major abbots, although it was not until the twentieth century that this claim would be fully — or almost fully — vindicated in practice.

On the whole, nevertheless, the Avignon years undermined the moral authority of the papacy and did grave harm to the Church. Burdensome taxes were levied by the Curia, Church offices were sold, luxurious living became the rule. Describing the papal court as "the Babylon of the West," the poet Petrarch fumed, "We seem to be among the kings of the Persians or Parthians, before whom we must fall down and worship, and who cannot be approached except presents be offered."

A terrible reckoning lay ahead. But first the Great Schism had to carry the weakening of the papacy and the internal damage to the Church to an extreme. If, humanly speaking, anything could have delivered the *coup de grace* to the papal office, it was the spectacle of two — and for a time three — men claiming to be pope while showering anathemas on their rivals.

The split began in 1378, the year after the end of the Avignon "captivity." Urban VI had just been chosen pope in a contentious election; some suspect he had become mentally unbalanced along the way. Whether that was so or not, a number of cardinals, chafing under his unexpectedly harsh rule, claimed that the pressure generated at the conclave by a Roman mob howling for an Italian pope invalidated the election. They proceeded to elect a new "pope" who took the name Clement VII and moved to Avignon.

The division was to last thirty-nine years. (A council at Pisa in 1409 tried to end it but made things worse by electing a third "pope.") At last the Council of Constance (1414-1418) managed to terminate the schism by accepting the resignation of one claimant (Gregory XII, considered to have been the authentic pope, whose legate was careful to read the assembly a bull convoking it as a general council before the resignation was announced), forcing another to resign, and declaring the third deposed. Martin V was then elected.

The Council of Constance has been called the most controversial of councils. It responded to a dire crisis, and it can hardly be blamed — quite the contrary — for that. Unfortunately, its rationale for what it did lent substance to two highly problematical ideas called Conciliarism and Gallicanism. Definitively rejected by the First and Second Vatican Councils, versions of both lately have reemerged in the primacy debate.

It is important to realize that Catholics who subscribed to Conciliarism and Gallicanism in the centuries when they flourished were not being disloyal; to suppose they were would mean applying a definitive clarification of the faith, achieved centuries later, to an earlier day. Many responsible individuals held these views; even now we should not overlook their elements of truth. But by the standard of faith it is clear today that neither was acceptable in the actual, historical form it took.

Fundamental to Conciliarism is the belief that a general, or ecumenical, council has authority separate from and superior to the authority of the pope. The Council of Constance in the decree *Haec Sancta* (April 6, 1415) said of itself that it was "lawfully assembled in the Holy Spirit, constitutes a General Council, represents the Catholic Church and has immediate power from Christ which anyone, of whatever status and condition, even if holding the Papal dignity, is bound to obey in matters pertaining to the Faith, extirpation of the schism and reformation of the said Church in head and members"; whoever refused to obey the council — including the pope, if it came to that — would be "subjected to appropriate penance and duly punished." (For those who may wonder: Constance was not a legitimately constituted general council able to define a doctrine at the time it issued *Haec Sancta*, since it was only *later* — before submitting his resignation — that Gregory XII convoked it; and *Haec Sancta* was in any case a legislative decree, not a statement of doctrine.) In the decree *Frequens* (October 9, 1497), Constance specified that a general council should be held every ten years.

There are two varieties of Conciliarism. The moderate version holds that a general council's authority is greater than the pope's in extraordinary circumstances like those the Council of Constance faced. If Church unity is gravely threatened, and the papacy can't act — if, in fact, the papacy itself is somehow implicated in the threat to unity — then God directly empowers the council to intervene, lest the "gates of hell" prevail against the Church. Radical Conciliarism holds that a general council routinely has authority over the pope. Cardinal Nicholas of Cusa, a leading conciliarist, wrote in 1440: "It does not appear that anything was said to Peter that implied any supremacy . . . all the apostles are equal in authority with Peter"; on this basis he argued that "the authority of enacting canons depends, not on the pope alone, but on common agreement."

Matters came to a head at the Council of Basel (1431-1449). Predictably clashing with Pope Eugene IV over papal authority, it proceeded to declare him deposed and elected an antipope, the duke of Savoy, who called himself Felix V. In the decree deposing Pope Eugene, the council asserted that "a General Council representing the Universal Church has its power immediately from Christ and . . . any one, of any dignity, even Papal, is bound to obey it."

Though dragging on for eighteen years, the assembly calling itself the Council of Basel was reduced long before the end to a schismatic rump group, Pope Eugene having transferred the site of the ecumenical council to Ferrara, where a new assembly convened on April 9, 1438. Known to history as the Council of Florence (or, sometimes, Basel/Ferrara/Florence/Rome), this council of reunion had a significant body of attendees from the Eastern Churches, among them the Byzantine emperor and the Patriarch of Constantinople. They preferred to parley with a council convoked by the Bishop of Rome rather than with the assembly in Basel.

The Council of Florence (1438-1445) taught on a number of disputed points dividing the Churches, with its teaching generally reflecting Western views. Desperate for political and military support from the West in their end-game struggle against the advancing Turks, the Easterners assented; but the reunion began to unravel soon after they returned home. The help expected from the West did not come, and in 1453 Constantinople fell. Embittered, the Byzantine Christians had no further interest in being united with their putative brothers in the West.

Nevertheless, Florence did produce an exceptionally clear and forceful statement of the doctrine of papal primacy — no less than a defined dogma.

> We likewise define that the holy Apostolic See, and the Roman Pontiff, hold the primacy throughout the entire world; and that the Roman Pontiff himself is the successor of blessed Peter, the chief of the Apostles, and the true vicar of Christ, and that he is the head of the entire Church, and the father and teacher of all Christians; and that full power was given to him in blessed Peter by our Lord Jesus Christ, to feed, rule, and govern the universal Church.

Meanwhile the "council" at Basel petered out, abandoned even by conciliarists like Nicholas of Cusa. At bottom, says historian William Henn, O.F.M. Cap., the conciliarists' failure reflected "the inherent insufficiency of any view which separates or even opposes the ecumenical council and the primacy. The one Church simply cannot have two distinct heads which can be opposed one against the other."

Gallicanism and the Reformation

But the harm had been done. Although the worst of it may have been to delay reform of the Church "in head and members" while popes and councils squabbled, almost as bad was the support lent by Conciliarism to the parallel movement called Gallicanism. Interacting and feeding off each other,

Conciliarism and Gallicanism entered the bloodstream of the Church where they would remain for many centuries — and where, in fact, they are once more circulating today.

At the heart of Gallicanism is a vision of autonomous national churches only loosely tied to Rome. In 1438 an assembly of French prelates and other "notables" convened by King Charles VII adopted, for promulgation by the king, a document known to history as the Pragmatic Sanction of Bourges. (In the late Roman empire a pragmatic sanction — *pragmatica sanctio* — was an imperial edict.) It declared the decisions of the Council of Basel to be law for the Church in France; henceforth the French Church would control appointments to ecclesiastical offices and other matters; and since, for practical purposes, the king controlled the French Church, it was clear who was chief beneficiary of the new arrangement.

Although, technically speaking, the claims of Bourges were set aside by a concordat signed in 1516 by Pope Leo X and King Francis I, the new document marked an even greater weakening of papal authority. "The greatest surrender of direct control which the papacy has ever made," one writer calls it. To the king — rather fatuously described as "wishing as a truly obedient son to follow our [the pope's] paternal advice" — and to his successors, the pope specifically concedes authority to nominate bishops and abbots, subject to confirmation by Rome. What the papacy had struggled over preceding centuries to gain was surrendered at the stroke of a pen.

These developments were part of a larger process, the emergence of the modern nation-state ruled by a strong central authority, then occurring many places in Europe. In the new political climate, at the end of the Middle Ages and the dawn of the modern era, papal claims to overarching authority in Christendom were increasingly irrelevant. The rise of the nation-states meant the rise of national churches.

The Reformation soon made that clear. To be sure, Martin Luther and the other Reformers were bitterly hostile to the papacy as a matter of principle. In *Against the Roman Papacy, an Institution of the Devil*, composed in 1546, the year of his death, Luther got to the core of the matter: "The Pope is the masked and incarnate devil because he is the antichrist." Even St. Francis de Sales, a gentle polemicist by the standards of the day, felt moved to remark, "You read the writings of Calvin, of Zwingle [Zwingli], of Luther: take out of these, I beg you, the railings, calumnies, insults, detraction, ridicule, and buffoonery which they contain against the Pope and the Holy See of Rome, and you will find that nothing will remain."

But the Reformers' anti-Romanism dovetailed with secular political currents. J. P. Kirsch points to the "growing self-consciousness of the State" and to the growing tendency, "owing to the close historical connection between the ecclesiastical and secular orders," for the state to encroach upon religion.

> The development of the State, in its modern form, among the Christian peoples of the West gave rise to many disputes between the clergy and laity, between bishops and the cities, between monasteries and the territorial lords. When the Reformers withdrew from the clergy all authority, especially all influence in civil affairs, they enabled the princes and municipal authorities to end these long-pending disputes to their own advantage by arbitrarily arrogating to themselves all disputed rights, banishing the hierarchy whose rights they usurped, and then establishing by their own authority a completely new ecclesiastical organization. The Reformed clergy thus possessed from the beginning only such rights as the civil authorities were pleased to assign them. Consequently the Reformed national churches were completely sub-

ject to the civil authorities, and the Reformers, who had entrusted to the civil power the actual execution of their principles, had now no means of ridding themselves of this servitude.

Meanwhile a parallel development, spurred by Conciliarism, Gallicanism, and a general tendency to resist Roman claims, was underway on the Catholic side of the new religious divide.

This was apparent even at the Council of Trent (1545-1563), which finally accomplished the long-deferred reform of the Church. Historians call it a "pope's council," and so it was in many ways. Determined, reform-minded popes kept it alive and on track against pressures to abandon the effort and vigorously spearheaded its implementation when it was over. But, that being so, why did Trent, which taught so much about so many challenged doctrines, not also teach on the subject of papal primacy, a doctrine at least as challenged as any?

The answer can be found in the fact that Tridentine popes, contemplating recent, painful history, felt themselves to be treading on thin ice in their relations with the bishops and concluded that it was safer to pass over primacy and related questions. Some at Trent held that bishops received authority to govern their local churches from the pope; others said episcopal authority came directly from Christ. The papal legates were instructed to steer the discussion away from such matters. The result was a notable gap in conciliar teaching.

Papal persistence in pushing Trent through to a successful conclusion nevertheless enhanced the papacy's prestige. So did the fact that responsibility for pursuing the council's reforms fell largely to single-minded postconciliar pontiffs like St. Pius V (pope from 1566 to 1572). It was helpful, too, that the new Society of Jesus, one of the most effective Catholic forces in the Counter-Reformation, was directly dependent on the papacy (select Jesuits even took a special fourth vow of loyalty to the pope). The ecclesiology of theologians like St. Robert Bellarmine, S.J., likewise had a strong papal focus, described by William Henn: "Christ is the head of the Church and the pope, as *vicarius Christi*, enjoys the supreme power of jurisdiction which comes to him from Christ through succession to the petrine ministry. His full pastoral power extends over all the faithful and their pastors. . . . Bellarmine sees in the pope the center and source of all ecclesial power." In defining the dogma of papal primacy, Vatican Council I was to agree with Bellarmine up to a point, but it did not go so far as to say that the pope is the source of all ecclesial power.

But even as the papal office once again was being exalted in theory, its real-world situation was greatly different. In the religious stalemate after the wars of religion, the papacy had to pay a high price for the political support of Catholic princes: no less than acceptance of their routine intervention in the affairs of the national churches. There is a notable expression of Gallicanism in, for instance, the "Four Articles Concerning Ecclesiastical Power," adopted by a French clergy congress of March, 1682, during a dispute between Louis XIV and Rome: "The rules, uses, and institutions generally received in the kingdom and the Gallican Church [shall] be maintained. . . . Although the pope has a chief voice in matters of faith . . . his judgment is not unalterable, except with the consent of the Church." Gallican ecclesiology was widely taken for granted. Many loyal Catholics thought this way.

Catholic religious nationalism was ratcheted up to a new, more virulent level by a book published in 1763. Called *The State of the Church and the Power of the Roman Pontiff*, the work was attributed to "Justinus Febronius," pseudonym of an auxiliary bishop of Trier, Johann Nikolaus von Hontheim. According to Febronius, the pope is first among the prelates of the Church but subordinate to the Church as a whole; primacy has to do only with essential rights exercised by Bishops of Rome in the first eight centuries, before the corrupting influence of the False Decretals was felt; primacy is not a power of jurisdiction but only of administering and unifying; the pope abuses his authority by condemning heretics, confirming bishops, establishing dioceses; he is not infallible; he is subordinate to an ecumenical council. Febronius advocates a general council and national synods to bring about reform, while exhorting rulers, with the cooperation of bishops, to reject papal decrees, refuse obedience to the pope where it can legitimately be refused, and tie the episcopacy closely to the state. Although condemned by Pope Clement XIII in 1764, Febronius's book had enormous influence.

Its thinking was carried even further in practice by Joseph II, Holy Roman Emperor from 1765 to 1790. The approach to the Church taken by this pious Catholic despot earns him a place in the line that includes Constantine, Justinian, Charlemagne, and other Caesaropapist rulers.

During his long reign, Emperor Joseph issued some six thousand decrees for the control and minute regulation of religion. With the cooperation of the bishops, he reorganized dioceses, specified how many Masses could be celebrated, seized Church schools and replaced them with state institutions, set up his own seminaries to train future priests, withdrew monasteries from papal control and dissolved them, and decided how many religious could reside in the empire. When Pius VI (pope from 1775 to 1799) traveled to Vienna in 1782 to remonstrate, the people greeted him with tumultuous enthusiasm; the Holy Roman Emperor received him politely and sent him home.

The emperor's brother Leopold, grand duke of Tuscany, also aspired to rule the Church. His theological adviser, Bishop

Scipio de Ricci, organized a diocesan synod at Pistoia in 1786 whose program on the antipapal Gallican model provoked a papal condemnation. There were similar developments elsewhere.

This also was an age when Catholic princes routinely exercised veto rights in papal elections. (As a matter of fact, this prerogative was invoked as late as the conclave of 1903, when Cardinal Mariano Rampolla, Secretary of State under Leo XIII, was vetoed by the emperor Franz Joseph. Apparently Cardinal Rampolla was a long shot anyway; be that as it may, the cardinals chose the Patriarch of Venice, Giuseppe Sarto, who took the name Pius X.) It was a time, too, when notables bombarded Rome with requests for ecclesiastical preferment for relatives and favorites. A writer who examined this voluminous correspondence in the Vatican archives suggests its flavor.

> The subject matter is furnished by the ambition to get deaneries, canonries, abbacies, bishoprics. One would imagine that not only the interested candidates were wide awake early every morning to take a survey of the situation, but that their fathers, their mothers (especially the fathers and mothers of baby candidates), all their brothers and all their sisters were taking in bulletins every day of the likely demise, the imminent death, the unhappy convalescence, the lucky departure at last, of bishop, canon, abbot, of all the enviable prebendaries visible betwixt the rising and the setting sun. Now it is not the post, the place, the duty, the vocation, that are thought of in the least. It is only the revenues. . . . Then a queen intervenes, or a king signifies his likings, and political relations are not to be despised. There are not wanting grave admonitions, which the supreme authority of the

Church directs shall be given, but in diplomatic style, to some crowned head or other; conveying what in plain terms means that it is none of his or her business, why such or such a person was appointed rather than some favorite.

This is amusing, up to a point; but there was nothing at all amusing about the suppression of the Society of Jesus. This draconian step was taken by Clement XIV on July 21, 1773, after long, intense pressure from the Catholic rulers of Catholic Europe. The Jesuits had made mistakes, sometimes been guilty of overreaching; but their suppression, having more to do with politics than religion, was a gesture of appeasement by a weakened papacy. Having noted the recent, brutal expulsions of Jesuits by order of the kings of France, Spain, Portugal, and the Two Sicilies, the papal decree adds: "But these same kings, our very dear sons in Jesus Christ, thought that this remedy could not be lasting in its effects or could not avail to tranquilize Christendom unless the society was altogether abolished and suppressed." It was a shameful hour for the papacy.

The Fall of the *Ancien Régime*

"Citizen Braschi, exercising the profession of Pontiff."

With that terse formula the prefect of Valence, France, recorded the death on August 29, 1799, of Pope Pius VI. Described as a "worthy but worldly" aristocrat, Giovanni Angelo Braschi had the misfortune to occupy the See of Peter during one of the most perilous episodes in Church history — the vast, volcanic explosion called the French Revolution. Elected in 1775, he failed to anticipate the calamity and was virtually helpless when it came.

The Church in France was convulsed by the Revolution. Some priests and religious sought to come to terms with the new order, even embraced it, while others gallantly resisted and paid with their lives. The mood of those who welcomed the Revolution is reflected in the Civil Constitution of the Clergy, drafted by Gallican members of the National Assembly and enacted on July 12, 1790: "No church or parish of France, and no French citizen, may, under any circumstances or on any pretext whatsoever, acknowledge the authority of an ordinary bishop or archbishop whose see is established under the name of a foreign power, or that of its delegates residing in France. . . . Appointments to bishoprics and curés are to be made by election only. . . . The new bishop may not apply to the pope for confirmation. . . . All bishops, *curés*, and officiating ministers . . . shall be furnished with suitable dwellings. . . . Salaries shall be assigned to all as indicated hereinafter."

About half the priests of France accepted the Civil Constitution but only seven bishops. A schismatic Constitutional Church then emerged, with bishops consecrated by the extraordinary Talleyrand, excommunicated former bishop of Autun, who had been an adviser to Louis XVI and would yet serve as foreign minister to the French Directory, to Napoleon, and finally to the Bourbons, whom he helped restore to the throne.

Before long, the Revolution turned on the Constitutional Church. Thirty thousand priests and bishops fled France, more than twenty thousand stayed and quit the priesthood, while the other five thousand or so suffered bloody persecution at the hands of an anti-Christian secular state.

In February, 1799, French troops entered Rome and seized Pius VI, then eighty-one and in poor health. Writing to the bishop of Valence on the two hundredth anniversary of Pius VI's death, John Paul II describes what happened next. "Seriously ill, he was torn from the See of Peter. Although he was able to enjoy a brief period of relative freedom in Florence, which allowed him to continue to exercise his responsibility as universal Pastor, he was forced to cross the Alps on snow-covered paths, and reached Briançon and then Valence, where death put an end to his earthly journey." John Paul calls the last months of Pius VI his Way of the Cross. Some supposed his death marked the end of the papacy and of the Church.

When Napoleon Bonaparte came to power in France, he had two aims especially in view: to restore order and to consolidate and enhance his own authority. To this nominal Catholic the Church looked like a useful tool for both purposes. "I am sure that the Catholic religion is the only religion that can make a stable community happy, and establish the foundations of good government," he explained. A working relationship with the new pope, Pius VII, was therefore necessary; and the latter's presence was required at the famous ceremony on December 2, 1804, in Notre Dame Cathedral when, taking from the altar crowns for himself and Josephine blessed by the pope, Napoleon performed the coronation by his own hand.

The most important events in the troubled relationship between the emperor and the pope concerned the reshaping of the French episcopate. As Napoleon wished, a concordat negotiated between the Holy See and the French Republic called for the naming of a fresh set of bishops, and, under pressure from the emperor, the pope complied. He persuaded forty-eight bishops to resign, deposed another thirty-seven, and named successors to them all. This "massacre of the apostles" was taken as a sign of papal weakness, and so it was. But it also was an extraordinary exercise of papal authority that wiped out the last of the Gallican power structure of the Church in France. Long years of pope-emperor conflict were to follow, including Pius VII's imprisonment at Fontainebleau; but even though hardly anyone suspected it, the seeds of the papacy's renewal had been sown.

After Napoleon's fall, Europe's statesmen busied themselves restoring a semblance of the old order. Since the papacy was part of it, the Papal States, seized by Napoleon, were restored to the pope. Still, no one any longer considered Rome a serious political player.

Painful though the popes of the day may have found that, it was to be a blessing. Despite the elaborate charade of putting the furniture back in place, the *ancien régime* — things as they'd been before the Revolution of 1789 — was gone forever. Its collapse had involved enormous suffering for the Church and the papacy. Yet the disappearance of the old system — with its Gallicanism and Febronianism and Josephenism, its unblushing interventions by emperors and kings in ecclesiastical affairs, its ceaseless mock-deferential attempts by Catholic princes to pressure the pope in their own interests — was to be immensely liberating.

The Revival of the Papacy

In 1799 a Camaldolese monk named Mauro Cappellari published a book called *The Triumph of the Holy See and the Church Over the Attacks of Innovators, Who Are Rejected and Fought With Their Own Weapons*. The volume refuted the Conciliarist and Gallicanist thinking of the day by arguing forcefully on behalf of papal infallibility and primacy. At the time, this must have seemed a last hurrah for a view of the papacy that had vanished forever. Hardly anyone would remember the book today, except for one thing: Having held various offices in the Camaldolese order, become a cardinal, and served with distinction as prefect of the Vatican congregation for missionary work, Mauro Cappellari in 1831 was elected pope. Taking the name Gregory XVI, he was to reign until 1846.

The pontificate of Gregory XVI marked the ascendancy of Ultramontanism. Especially associated with this movement that brought about an astonishing rehabilitation of the papacy were Joseph de Maistre ("Christianity rests entirely on the pope") and Félicité de Lamennais. The word Ultramontanism comes from two Latin words (*ultra montes*) meaning "beyond the mountains," the mountains in question being the Alps, and "beyond" usually taken as pointing southward — toward Rome.

In a sense, every faithful Roman Catholic is an Ultramontanist, inasmuch as he or she regards the papacy a gift of God to the Church and wishes to respond appropriately to the exercise of papal teaching and governing authority, in the spirit of Vatican Council II:

> In order that the episcopate itself . . . might be one and undivided [Christ] put Peter at the head of the other apostles, and in him he set up a lasting and visible source and foundation of the unity both of faith and of communion. This teaching concerning the institution, the permanence, the nature and import of the sacred primacy of the Roman Pontiff and his infallible teaching office, the sacred synod proposes anew to be firmly believed by all the faithful.
>
> *Lumen Gentium*, 18

These days, though, the terms Ultramontanism and Ultramontanist often are used pejoratively to signify a tendency to look to Rome for decisions in situations where local churches and individuals should trust their own prudence, maturity of faith, and prayerful discernment of God's will. Blaming Protestants and Gallicanists for making Ultramontanism an opprobrious term, Umberto Benigni said flatly, "Ultramontanism and Catholicism are the same thing." Unfortunately, Monsignor Benigni's role in the so-called "white terror" accompanying the campaign against Modernism early in the twentieth century (he headed a secret society that specialized in collecting information on Modernists and suspected Modernists and reporting them to the authorities) does not set his version of Ultramontanism in a particularly favorable light.

But all this lay in the future. In the middle years of the nineteenth century, Ultramontanism was spearheading a remarkable revival of the papacy.

Gregory XVI was succeeded in 1846 by Blessed Pius IX. His pontificate of thirty-two years was not only history's longest up to now but one of the most turbulent and influential. A man of warm and winning personality whom the Church may one day declare a saint, Pius IX was one of the most loved popes ever as well as one of the most deeply disliked.

The revival of the papacy's spiritual stature coincided with a precipitous decline of its temporal power. For centuries, it had been taken for granted that the pope had to rule some reasonably substantial territory in order to be independent; for him to be the subject of another ruler would be intolerable. But the Italian nationalist movement, often bitterly anticlerical, swallowed up the Papal States and eventually, in 1870, Rome itself. The calamity forced the suspension of Vatican Council I and moved Pius IX to adopt the role of "Prisoner of the Vatican" that his successors would maintain until well into the twentieth century.

Although most people at the time considered the loss of the Papal States a disaster for the papacy — applauded by some, deplored by others — not everybody agreed. In the United States, the social philosopher and writer Orestes Brownson, a convert to Catholicism, suggested that American Catholics could teach their European coreligionists a thing or two about Church-State relations. Alfred Austin, Queen Victoria's poet laureate, said bluntly, "Never in its history of so many centuries has such a stroke of good fortune befallen the Papacy as the abolition of its Temporal Power." And the papacy's "shrewdest councillors" were aware of the fact, he added, even though they could not say so publicly.

> Only the other day, I was walking in the Vatican Gardens with a well-known English Roman Catholic who lives in Rome, and he confirmed me in this suspicion. . . . The Protest against Spoliation, for spoliation of course it was, is still maintained, for certain diplomatic and likewise certain financial reasons. But it grows fainter and fainter, and will in time, without explicit disavowal, die away; and then the Papacy, the true Heir of the Caesars and the Pax Romana, will, I believe, be stronger than ever.

One must admire the laureate's foresight.

Today Pius IX is remembered for his profound antipathy to the antireligious thrust of nineteenth-century European liberalism and the rising secularism of the day. He laid out his position in documents like the 1864 encyclical *Quanta Cura* and the accompanying "Syllabus of Errors" condemning "the particular errors of our age." But far and away the most notable event of the pontificate for the papal office itself was the definition by the First Vatican Council (1869-1870) of the dogmas of papal primacy and papal infallibility.

The First Vatican Council

Vatican I's teaching on primacy and infallibility is found in *Pastor Aeternus*, the Dogmatic Constitution on the Church of Christ, which the council adopted on July 18, 1870.

The vote in favor of papal infallibility was 533 to 2. Although fifty-seven bishops, opposed to defining the dogma on grounds of opportuneness or substance, left Rome the day before rather than vote no, the definition did not cover as many exercises of the pope's teaching authority as some Ultra-montanists had hoped it would do, a fact quickly pointed out by John Henry Newman, himself a prominent inopportunist.

The council's teaching on papal primacy is found in chapters one, two, and three of *Pastor Aeternus* after an introductory statement. (Note that these "chapters" run only a few hundred words each.)

Chapter one concerns the institution of primacy in Peter: "We teach and declare that according to the testimonies of the Gospel the primacy of jurisdiction over the entire Church of God was promised and was conferred immediately and directly upon the blessed Apostle Peter by Christ the Lord." The customary New Testament texts (Matthew 16:17ff., John 21:15ff.) are cited.

The chapter closes with a "canon" anathematizing the view contrary to what the council is teaching. This has been the practice of many general councils and is intended to identify with maximum clarity just what is being taught. The canon here reads: "If anyone says that the blessed Apostle Peter was not established by the Lord Christ as the chief of all the apostles, and the visible head of the whole militant Church, or, that the same received great honor but did not receive from the same our Lord Jesus Christ directly and immediately the primacy in true and proper jurisdiction: let him be anathema." In other words, the primacy was instituted by Christ, it was conferred by him on St. Peter as head of the apostles and visible head of the Church on earth, and it was *not* a primacy of honor but of jurisdiction.

Chapter two is concerned with the perpetuity of primacy. The primacy Christ instituted and conferred on Peter does not end with Peter but is permanent. "[It] must endure always in the Church which was founded upon a rock and will endure firm until the end of the ages. . . . Therefore, whoever succeeds

Peter in this chair, he according to the institution of Christ himself, holds the primacy of Peter over the whole Church." On this point the council quotes St. Leo the Great (pope from 440 to 461), St. Irenaeus (c. 130-c. 200), and St. Ambrose (c. 340-397). Leo: "Blessed Peter persevering in the accepted fortitude of the rock does not abandon the guidance of the Church which he has received." Irenaeus: "It has always been necessary because of mightier preeminence for every church to come to the Church of Rome." Ambrose: The see of Rome is the source of the "venerable communion" of those who belong to the universal Church.

Chapter two's canon reads: "If anyone then says that it is not from the institution of Christ the Lord Himself, or by divine right, that the blessed Peter has perpetual successors in the primacy over the universal Church, or that the Roman Pontiff is not the successor of blessed Peter in the same primacy, let him be anathema." In other words, the primacy of jurisdiction — the power to govern the universal Church — conferred by Christ on Peter, is transmitted in perpetuity to Peter's successors, the popes.

Chapter three presents the council's teaching on the power of papal primacy and the manner of its exercise. Having reaffirmed the Council of Florence's definition of the dogma of primacy, it continues:

> Furthermore We teach and declare that the Roman Church, by the disposition of the Lord, holds the sovereignty of ordinary power over all others, and that this power of jurisdiction on the part of the Roman Pontiff, which is truly episcopal [the power a bishop has], is immediate [not exercised only through other bishops or rulers]; and with respect to this the pastors and the faithful of whatever rite and dignity, both as separate indi-

viduals and all together, are bound by the duty of hierarchical subordination and true obedience, not only in things which pertain to faith and morals, but also in those which pertain to the discipline and government of the Church spread over the whole world, so that the Church of Christ, protected not only by the Roman Pontiff, but by the unity of communion as well as of the profession of the same faith is one flock under the one highest shepherd.

Reading just this much, someone might ask: If this is true of the pope, what is left for the bishops? Anticipating the question, Vatican I immediately adds:

This power of the Supreme Pontiff is so far from interfering with that power of ordinary and immediate episcopal jurisdiction by which the bishops . . . as true shepherds individually feed and rule the individual flocks assigned to them, that the same [power] is asserted, confirmed, and vindicated by the supreme and universal shepherd.

In other words: No power struggles between pope and bishops, but complementarity and collaboration instead.

Pastor Aeternus then returns to the pope, declaring that in exercising primacy, he has the right to communicate freely with pastors and faithful. "We condemn and disapprove the opinions of those who say that this communication of the supreme head with pastors and flocks can lawfully be checked, or who make this so submissive to secular power that they contend that whatever is established by the Apostolic See or its authority for the government of the Church has no force or value unless confirmed by an order of the secular power." So much for the claims of Gallicanist churchmen and Catholic princes that it was for them to decide whether Rome's voice would be heard in their territories.

Next the constitution declares that the pope is "the supreme judge of the faithful" whose judgments the faithful have a right to seek. Moreover: "The judgment of the Apostolic See . . . is to be disclaimed by no one, nor is anyone permitted to pass judgment on its judgment." So it follows that "they stray from the straight path of truth who affirm that it is permitted to appeal from the judgments of the Roman Pontiffs to an ecumenical Council, as to an authority higher than the Roman Pontiff." So much for the claims of Conciliarism.

Chapter three concludes with this canon:

> If anyone thus speaks, that the Roman Pontiff has only the office of inspection or direction, but not the full and supreme power of jurisdiction over the universal Church, not only in things which pertain to faith and morals, but also in those which pertain to the discipline and government of the Church spread over the whole world; or, that he possesses only the more important parts, but not the whole plenitude of this supreme power; or that this power of his is not ordinary and immediate, or over the churches altogether and individually, and over the pastors and the faithful altogether and individually: let him be anathema.

Some people complain because *Pastor Aeternus* stated the dogma of papal primacy in legal terms and used the word "jurisdiction." To some extent, this is a matter of taste. But it is also something more, since there are both advantages and disadvantages in this use of juridical language. On the one hand, it is clear and precise, and clarity and precision obviously are desirable in defining dogmas to be held as matters of faith. On the other hand, legal language can have secular connotations that are undesirable and even misleading in an ecclesial context. Whatever else might be said of the jurisdiction of the pope, it is by no means the same as the jurisdiction of a secular ruler.

Today, instead of jurisdiction, many people prefer to speak of the ministry or service of the pope and the bishops. "The holders of office, who are invested with a sacred power, are, in fact, dedicated to promoting the interests of their brethren," says Vatican Council II (*Lumen Gentium*, 18). Like the older legal language, the language of service offers advantages to someone seeking to understand papal primacy; but it too has drawbacks. That is especially the case if it becomes separated in people's minds from authority and jurisdiction. Papal primacy is a ministry of service whose essence is the power to exercise supreme, universal, immediate jurisdiction everywhere in the Church. How the service should be rendered — how the power should be used — is the question.

Looking for a way around the teaching of Vatican I, would-be tamers of the pope sometimes claim that the council didn't act freely. It is said — for example, by the Catholic writer Garry Wills, in a recent book accusing the papacy of systematic, systemic dishonesty — that Pius IX and the Roman Curia put so much pressure on the bishops that the definitions of primacy and infallibility do not count. But this is fantasy; even Hans Küng, in his book attempting to deconstruct infallibility, agrees that it "cannot be maintained." The fact that fifty-seven bishops opposed to defining infallibility were free to pack up and leave Rome hardly suggests coercion. Certainly some council Fathers (Archbishop, later Cardinal, Henry Edward Manning of Westminster is a notable example) worked hard for a strong affirmation of papal authority; so did Pius IX. But, says Klaus Schatz, it "ignores the facts" to attribute the outcome to pressure. In fact, most bishops came to Rome convinced of the truth of these dogmas, and "the definitions . . . were more the natural result of a long process of historical development than the product of deliberate political manipulations."

Pastor Aeternus affirms the authority of the episcopacy and disavows the idea of a power struggle. Still, some have contended that Vatican I made bishops mere creatures of the papacy; and the council surely did couch its statement of papal authority in terms both strong and somewhat one-sided.

An unintended test case of Vatican I's intentions arose in 1872 when Chancellor Bismarck instructed German diplomats, in the wake of the council, not to waste time dealing with bishops but to take their business directly to the pope. The German bishops protested. They rejected Bismarck's claims that, as a result of Vatican I, "episcopal jurisdiction has been absorbed into the papal" and the pope had "in principle taken the place of each individual bishop," while bishops were reduced to "tools of the Pope." On the contrary, they said, "It is in virtue of the same divine institution upon which the papacy rests that the episcopate also rests." Pius IX commended the German bishops for their stand and confirmed that they had expressed "the true meaning of the Vatican Council."

The Second Vatican Council

"In theology the question of papal primacy was so much in the foreground that the Church appeared essentially as a centrally directed institution which one was dogged in defending but which only encountered one externally." This is how Cardinal Ratzinger describes the state of things prevailing in Catholicism for some decades after Vatican I. At times, the mindset of centralization expressed itself in an extreme form; as when, for example, the bishop of Strasbourg, France, in 1943 declared the pope to be not only "the supreme head of the

Church" but "first bishop of the diocese of Strasbourg." Others probably thought like that, too, and, considering they did, one can only take it to be a special grace of a merciful God that in the twentieth century the Church was blessed with popes who not only were strong leaders but conscientious ones.

Even so, there were those who were convinced that some balancing — by teaching about the bishops' authority — would eventually be needed for the good of the Church. Pope John XXIII's surprise 1959 announcement of an ecumenical council provided these bishops and theologians with the opportunity. It seems that not a few Fathers of Vatican II felt it their main job to balance Vatican I's teaching on papal primacy with teaching on the collegiality of bishops associating them with the pope in the governance of the universal Church.

But there was hardly unanimity about that. In a straw vote on October 30, 1963, during the council's second session, the bishops were presented with several propositions. One stated that the College of Bishops — the body of the world's bishops in union with the pope — was successor to the College of Apostles; and, together with the pope and never apart from him, his primacy over bishops and faithful remaining fully intact, this episcopal college enjoyed full and supreme power over the universal Church. According to another proposition, full and supreme power belonged to the College of Bishops, in union with its head, the pope, by divine right. The first proposition was adopted 1,808 to 336, the second 1,717 to 408. While these were very strong majorities in favor of collegiality, in the context of the council negative votes of 336 and 408 were substantial minorities.

Some consider the most important struggle of Vatican II to have been one over collegiality that took place mostly out of sight. Not surprisingly, the final text of the Dogmatic Constitution on the Church, *Lumen Gentium*, contains both clarifications and compromises regarding this doctrine. That is especially true of the "Explanatory Note" attached to the text, which was drafted by the council's Theological Commission at the direction of Pope Paul; the note makes it clear that episcopal collegiality is to be understood in a moderate, not radical, sense fully recognizing the unimpeded primacy of the pope. The bishops approved this by a vote of 2,099 to 46; on November 19, 1964, near the end of the third session, they adopted *Lumen Gentium*, 2,134 to 10.

Vatican II's ecclesiological teaching is found mainly in *Lumen Gentium*. That makes the constitution in some respects the council's most important document, establishing the basis for the discussion of other, particular topics (for example, bishops, laity, ecumenism) in other conciliar documents.

The doctrine on the pope and episcopal college is contained in chapter three of *Lumen Gentium*, "The Church Is Hierarchical."

It begins by reaffirming the teaching of Vatican I regarding the primacy and infallibility of the pope: "This teaching . . . the sacred synod [Vatican II] proposes anew to be firmly believed by all the faithful." Having made that clear, the council then states its further intention: "to proclaim publicly and enunciate clearly the doctrine concerning bishops, successors of the apostles, who together with Peter's successor the Vicar of Christ and the visible head of the whole Church, direct the house of the living God."

Christ is said to have organized the apostles as "a college or permanent assembly," headed by Peter, and to have given them the mission of teaching, sanctifying, and governing the Church. Since this mission is "destined to last until the end of the world (cf. Mt. 28.20)," the apostles named successors, and the successors named successors, and that will continue until the end of time. This is the apostolic succession of the bishops, who have "by divine institution taken the place of the apostles as pastors of the Church." Consecration as a bishop confers on a man the "fullness of the sacrament of Orders," including the office of teaching, sanctifying, and governing; but these functions "of their very nature can be exercised only in hierarchical communion with the head and members of the college" — in communion, that is, with the pope and the other bishops.

Citing again the "collegiate character and structure of the episcopal order," as illustrated in the holding of ecumenical councils, *Lumen Gentium* next declares the unique authority of the pope.

> The college or body of bishops has . . . no authority unless united with the Roman Pontiff, Peter's successor, as its head, whose primatial authority . . . over all, whether pastors or faithful, remains in its integrity. For the Roman Pontiff, by reason of his office as Vicar of Christ, namely, and as pastor of the entire Church, has full, supreme and universal power over the whole Church, a power which he can always exercise unhindered.

And the bishops?

> The order of bishops is the successor to the college of the apostles in their role as teachers and pastors, and in it the apostolic college is perpetuated. Together with their head, the Supreme Pontiff, and never apart from him, they have supreme and full authority over the universal Church; but this power cannot be exercised without the agreement of the Roman Pontiff.

This section of the constitution closes with further words about the episcopal college.

In it the bishops, whilst loyally respecting the primacy and preeminence of their head, exercise their own proper authority for the good of their faithful, indeed even for the good of the whole Church. . . . The supreme authority over the whole Church, which this college possesses, is exercised in a solemn way in an ecumenical council. There never is an ecumenical council which is not confirmed or at least recognized as such by Peter's successor. And it is the prerogative of the Roman Pontiff to convoke such councils, to preside over them and to confirm them.

The bishops, dispersed around the world and in union with the pope, also can exercise the "same collegiate power," provided the pope asks them to do so or at least recognizes what they do as a "truly collegiate act."

Lumen Gentium then sketches the outlines of the *communio* ecclesiology so prominent since Vatican II in discussions of the nature and structure of the Church (we shall look more closely at it below). Special emphasis is placed on the pope and bishops. This understanding of the Church underscores the importance of "particular" or "local" churches (usually understood as dioceses and other dioceselike jurisdictions, although the expression sometimes refers to the Church at the national level — "the French Church," "the Polish Church," and the like — or at the grassroots level; at this point in the Constitution on the Church, the focus clearly is on dioceses).

The Roman Pontiff . . . is the perpetual and visible source and foundation of the unity both of the bishops and of the whole company of the faithful. The individual bishops are the visible source and foundation of unity in their own particular Churches, which are constituted after the model of the universal Church; it is in these and out of them that the one and unique Catholic Church exists.

Lumen Gentium explains that the primary pastoral responsibility of bishops is to "exercise their pastoral office over the portion of the People of God assigned to them [that is, over their own dioceses], not over other Churches nor the Church universal." As members of the episcopal college, bishops should indeed have "care and solicitude" for the whole Church; this is not expressed by "any act of jurisdiction," however, but by promoting the unity of the faith, teaching the faithful to expand their concerns to take in the entire Mystical Body, and promoting apostolates common to the whole Church. The importance of supporting the missions is affirmed; so is the legitimate diversity of liturgies, theologies, and spiritual traditions in the various Eastern churches and rites, as well as (a little incongruously, perhaps, just here in the document) the value of bishops' conferences.

Sections 24 and 25 of the constitution deal with the teaching office, including papal infallibility and the infallibility of the "ordinary magisterium" or teaching authority of bishops, in union with the pope and dispersed throughout the world. Section 26 returns to *communio* ecclesiology, now considered at the grassroots: "This Church of Christ is really present in all legitimately organized local groups of the faithful. . . . In them the faithful are gathered together through the preaching of the Gospel of Christ, and the mystery of the Lord's Supper is celebrated." But, naturally, "every legitimate celebration of the Eucharist is regulated by the bishop," who is responsible for overseeing the administration of all the sacraments in his diocese.

Section 27 speaks of the bishops' authority to govern their particular churches. It makes important points about the relationship of their authority to papal authority.

> This power, which they exercise personally in the name of Christ, is proper, ordinary and immediate, although its exercise is ultimately controlled by the supreme authority of the Church and can be confined within certain limits should the usefulness of the Church and the faithful require that. . . . The pastoral charge, that is, the permanent and daily care of their sheep, is entrusted to them fully; nor are they to be regarded as vicars of the Roman Pontiff; for they exercise the power which they possess in their own right. . . . Consequently their authority, far from being damaged by the supreme and universal power, is much rather defended, upheld and strengthened by it.

The rest of the chapter speaks of priests and deacons in relation to bishops.

In presenting the "Explanatory Note" appended to *Lumen Gentium* (November 16, 1964), the secretary general of the council said: "It is according to the mind and sense of this note that the teaching contained in chapter three is to be explained and understood." It makes these points:

The word "college" does not have a "strictly juridical sense," as if referring to equals who turn over their powers to a chairman. In *Lumen Gentium*, it refers to "a permanent body whose form and authority is to be ascertained from revelation."

A bishop becomes a member of the college through episcopal consecration and "hierarchical communion" with its head and members, and this episcopal consecration confers an "ontological share in the sacred functions" of bishops. In order to exercise his power, however, a bishop must be appointed to some office "according to norms approved by the supreme authority." As for communion, it is not "some vague sort of *goodwill*, but as *something organic* which calls for a juridical structure."

There is "no such thing as the college without its head" — a point said to need emphasizing "lest the fullness of the Pope's power be jeopardized." The relevant distinction here is not between the body of bishops and the pope, as if the former could exist without the latter, but between the body of bishops together with the pope and the pope alone. It is up to the pope to decide what he will do in light of the Church's needs at any given time.

And, finally, the college is not always engaged in collegiate activity but does so only "occasionally" and with the consent of its head, lacking which "the bishops cannot act as a college."

In a review of several recent books that were published as part of the primacy debate, Avery Dulles speaks of an interpretation of the Second Vatican Council that he sees as "probably dominant among the Catholic intelligentsia of Western Europe and North America." It is "that the minority at Vatican II prevented the majority from fully succeeding in their laudable efforts at reform." Of this Father Dulles remarks: "It might be more correct to hold that the minority enabled the council to maintain proper continuity with the Catholic tradition."

The First and Second Vatican Councils contain much doctrine on the pope and the bishops. Papal primacy and episcopal collegiality both are affirmed. Despite a tendency in some circles to complain about one or the other, Catholics ought to welcome both.

Still, it would be naïve to think everything about the relationship primacy and collegiality has been settled. There are many outstanding questions. At the 1996 theological symposium on primacy organized by the Congregation for the Doctrine of the Faith, William Henn summarized the "official doctrine" up to this point.

> It has affirmed the divine origin both of the primacy and of the episcopacy within the Church. It has rejected any radical opposition between the two. It has asserted that the college of bishops needs a head to serve as principle of unity and of coordination. It has taught that the primacy is rooted in the personal promise to Peter and to his successors so that they might serve the collective unity of the episcopacy and of the whole Church. It has proposed as necessary to such personal primacy the freedom to effectively foster the unity of the Church as a whole, in such a way that this freedom is not legally conditioned by the approval of the episcopacy. It has affirmed that the primacy is bound to respect and collaborate with the episcopacy, which also is divinely established by Christ for the well-being of the Church. It has taught that both the college of bishops, as a whole together with their head, and the primate, as head, have an obligation and right to care for the unity of the Church as a whole. It has affirmed the sacramentality of the episcopacy and thereby the dignity of each individual bishop as a vicar of Christ in such a way that the primacy does not and cannot diminish that dignity. It has proposed that the primacy and the episcopacy are bound together by ties of hierarchical communion. It has not explained precisely how all of these principles function together nor the range of diversity possible in the actual exercise of the relation between primacy and episcopacy.

That, by and large, is how matters now stand.

CHAPTER THREE

The Case for Taming the Pope

The hopeful energy of the Second Vatican Council, or Vatican II, as it came to be called, appears to many a spent force. The church of Pius XII is reasserting itself in confirmation of a pyramidal church model: faith in the primacy of the man in the white robe dictating in solitude from the pinnacle. . . . A future titanic struggle between the progressives and the traditionalists is in prospect, with the potential for a cataclysmic schism.

John Cornwell
Hitler's Pope

Did the policies and personality of Pius XII (pope from 1939 to 1958) contribute to the rise of Adolf Hitler? In *Hitler's Pope*, a book published in 1999, British journalist John Cornwell argues they did. The Church may one day declare Pope Pius a saint, and Cornwell does not claim he was an evil man or an admirer of Hitler and the Nazis; he paints a picture of a conscientious churchman in anguish over the hatred and violence around him. Still, he contends that Pius's view of the papacy, and the steps he took to further it as Vatican diplomat, Secretary of State, and finally pope, helped bring Hitler to power and keep him there.

Cornwell writes: "Pacelli, whose canonization process is now well advanced, has become the icon . . . of those traditionalists who read and revise the provisions of the Second Vatican Council from the viewpoint of Pacelli's ideology of papal power — an ideology that has proved disastrous in the century's history." In pursuit of highly centralized Roman authority, he argues, Eugenio Pacelli, as nuncio to Bavaria and later all Germany, hewed to a policy line which so gravely weakened the Church in Germany that it couldn't stand up to the Nazis.

In this story, the collapse of German Catholicism under pressure from Hitler and his thugs is contrasted with the successful resistance of nineteenth-century German Catholics to Bismarck's *Kulturkampf* (culture war) against the Church. The difference is said to lie in the strong and relatively autonomous network of church-related institutions and programs possessed by those Catholics of earlier days, which was undermined by the concordat Pacelli negotiated with Hitler for the sake of his Rome-centered policy. The lesson, Cornwell contends, is that local autonomy must replace "Roman centralizing" in the Church of the twenty-first century — or else. Commenting on this thesis, Nicholas Lash, emeritus professor of theology at Cambridge, says: "It is not the business of the papacy to *run* the Catholic Church."

Historians will have to settle the argument about what contribution, if any, policies pursued by Pius XII may have made to the rise of Hitler, but it is clear that *Hitler's Pope* is a very dubious piece of work in its facts and its interpretations. Kenneth L. Woodward, veteran religion writer for *Newsweek*, calls it "a classic example of what happens when an ill-equipped journalist assumes the airs of sober scholarship" — a warning many of us might well take to heart. Nevertheless, Cornwell's thesis is interesting here for a particular reason: This is pope-taming with a vengeance.

But that is getting ahead of the story.

Rationales for Decentralization

John Cornwell's attack on Pius XII hardly exhausts the arguments for decentralizing authority in the Church. Other rationales range from the moderate and well-reasoned to the ideological and impassioned. In this chapter we shall look at several of these arguments and, for the most part, let them speak for themselves. What *is* the case for taming the pope — or, in less confrontational terms, for a large-scale program of decentralization in the Catholic Church?

As we have seen, one reason for pressing this question concerns the need for answers to various ecclesiological questions in the wake of Vatican Council I and Vatican Council II. These questions have to do with, among other things, the relationship between the pope and the college of bishops — that is to say, they concern the practical implications of collegiality — and also with the relationship between the universal Church and the particular, or local, churches.

At the 1996 Roman symposium organized by the Congregation for the Doctrine of the Faith, theologian Michael J. Buckley, S.J., argued that both "primacy" and "episcopate" should be understood first of all as "relations" — of the pope to the bishops, and of the bishops to one another and to the other members of the Church. "One cannot understand the primacy adequately without understanding what is the real character of the unity of the episcopate," Father Buckley said. No doubt this is true, just as the episcopal office and the episcopal college can't be fully understood apart from the pope and papal primacy. These relationships need exploring, as does the question of how they are best expressed.

A second rationale reflects ecumenical concerns. In 1967, Pope Paul VI said: "The pope, as we all know, is undoubtedly the gravest obstacle in the path of ecumenism." He didn't mean the person of the pope or any one pope in particular, but the papal office — which, nevertheless, was meant to be "an indispensable source of truth, charity, and unity." Of course, for some non-Catholic Christians the only acceptable approach to the papacy would be to abolish it; but, those aside, others object not so much to the office as to the way it is, or has been, exercised. Archbishop Quinn makes a great deal of this ecumenical fact of life in his Oxford paper and his book.

Pope John Paul recognized the problem in *Ut Unum Sint*, as he had done before. On the one hand, he says, the pope's title "servant of the servants of God" is a safeguard against separating power from service in the Petrine ministry. "On the other hand, as I acknowledged on the important occasion of a visit to the World Council of Churches in Geneva on June 12, 1984, the Catholic Church's conviction that in the ministry of the Bishop of Rome she has preserved, in fidelity to the apostolic Tradition and the faith of the Fathers, the visible sign and guarantor of unity, constitutes a difficulty for most other Christians, whose memory is marked by certain painful recollections. To the extent that we are responsible for these, I join my Predecessor Paul VI in asking forgiveness." Hence the satisfaction he took from the fact that "the question of the primacy of the Bishop of Rome has now become a subject of study" in ecumenical circles.

Such papal affirmations lead Hermann Pottmeyer, a German theologian and member of the International Theological Commission, to suggest that *Ut Unum Sint* may some day be seen as launching "a new era in the history of Christianity." Perhaps so; but whether that era will, or should, be marked by the papacy's transformation into "an ecumenical Petrine ministry" (Father Pottmeyer's term) isn't so clear.

Antipapal sentiment is a third source of the impetus for pope-taming. Adrian Fortescue once expressed dismay about those people who "start from a fundamental principle that, if the Pope is down on any mortal thing, that thing must be right." Presumably he meant non-Catholics, but these days some Catholics apparently feel the same. In fact, Hans Urs von Balthasar speaks of a "deep-seated anti-Roman attitude," always more or less present in some sectors of the Church, that has to be "overcome again and again by the community." Moreover, he adds, in modern times some Catholics have been moved to "demonstrate their Christian 'adulthood' " by "arrogant and even venomous superiority to all that comes from Rome, happens in Rome or goes to Rome."

It could be that John Cornwell exhibits some of this generic anti-Roman sentiment. If so, he has company. Bernard Häring complains of "monarchical — even at times absolutistic — structures, worldly trappings, triumphalistic pomp and ridiculous titles of honor" assumed by Rome since Constantine; others indulge in similar rhetoric. At a time when good-mannered Protestants, moved by ecumenical tact as well as ordinary civility, have abandoned anti-Roman polemics, some Catholics have picked up where the sons and daughters of the Reformation left off.

Von Balthasar remarks that the critics sometimes take the line, "The papacy but not this pope." In other words, the office is acceptable, but its current occupant is not. It is a variation on this to lavish praise on one pope in order to denigrate another. For example, Hans Küng on the *Hitler's Pope* controversy: "Pius XII does not deserve canonization, whereas John XXIII does not need it." Back in the 1970s, when von Balthasar wrote, progressives often compared Paul VI to John XXIII, to the disadvantage of the former. Lately, they've compared John Paul II to Paul VI — to *John Paul's* disadvantage.

A fourth reason why progressive Catholics want decentralization is the belief that it will smooth the path for changes they desire in Church doctrine and discipline. It is hardly a secret what these are. At Oxford, Archbishop Quinn spoke of issues he said were "closed to discussion" at present: women's ordination, general absolution, the celibacy of the clergy, and others. (The list is missing from his book.)

Archbishop Quinn presented his issues tentatively, as matters needing to be aired. Others are more blunt. The International Movement We Are Church, a coalition claiming to represent one hundred twenty-seven groups of "disaffected Catholics" (the phrase is that of the Reuters news agency) in twenty-seven countries, says it collected two and a half million signatures in 1997 on a petition to the Vatican containing the following "five demands."

1. "Building a Church of brothers and sisters that recognizes the equality of all the baptized, including the inclusion of the People of God in the election of bishops in their local churches."

2. "Equal rights for men and women, including the admission of women to all Church ministries."

3. "Free choice of either a celibate or married life for all those who dedicate themselves to the service of the Church."

4. "A positive attitude toward sexuality, and a recognition of personal conscience in decision-making."

5. "A message of joy and not condemnation, including dialogue, freedom of speech and thought. No anathemas and no exclusion as a means of solving problems, especially as this applies to theologians."

People who may not be acquainted with this code language should be aware that a program of radical change lies behind the bland words. It includes ordaining women as priests, accepting contraception and homosexual sex, tolerating systematic theological dissent, and democratizing Church governance. (In October, 1999, during a synod of European bishops held in Rome, We Are Church issued a detailed set of demands on such matters as contraception, divorce and remarriage, ordaining women priests, and ending priestly celibacy.)

The Ecclesiology of *Communio*

As this overview suggests, the current pressure for devolution comes from a number of sources. All should be taken seriously, although for different reasons. That is particularly so, as Pope John Paul points out, of the ecumenical rationale, as well as the rationale reflecting important questions about primacy and collegiality in the wake of Vatican I and Vatican II.

In his history of primacy, Klaus Schatz says the legacy of the two councils includes two different visions of the Church's essential structure — two ecclesiologies — not yet integrated up to now. Vatican I's is said to be an "ecclesiology of *jurisdictio*" — jurisdiction — whereas Vatican II embraced "the still older and now rediscovered ecclesiology of *communio*." Although "placed side by side," Father Schatz contends, the two ecclesiologies "remain unconnected." Unless they are integrated in a new synthesis, the result could be a return to a "purely monarchical ecclesiology," with no room for collegiality or for the approach he particularly favors, a kind of neo-Conciliarism that would be consistent with the teaching of Vatican I.

One need not hold that neo-Conciliarism really would be good for the Church in order to agree that, to integrate the two ways of thinking about the Church, some large matters will have to be addressed. For example:

What is the role of the college of bishops and of individual bishops at the level of the universal Church? How should these roles be expressed institutionally?

What is the role of bishops at the national level? What authority should national conferences of bishops have?

How participatory should the governance of the Church be, at all levels? What structures and processes are needed at the local, regional, and national levels and the level of the universal Church, for nonbishops to play their appropriate roles?

Answers will come from working out the implications of the ecclesiology of *communio*.

Whatever else *communio* means, it does *not* mean a people's Church where papal primacy is a symbolic primacy of honor. Sometimes it is said that in the first millennium "primacy of honor" meant real authority, not just a symbolic role. But if it did, then the first-millennium primacy wasn't what is now called primacy of honor but primacy of jurisdiction by another name; in which case it isn't helpful now to speak of "primacy of honor" — which has come to mean something quite different — as if it pointed to a happy solution with historical roots.

Theologians and others have taken up *communio* ecclesiology enthusiastically in the last two decades. This troubles some extremely conservative Catholics, who believe the view of the Church as *communio* has more to do with Orthodox "eucharistic" ecclesiology than with a traditional Roman Catholic understanding. Yet this way of thinking of the Church has much to recommend it. It reflects the fact that the Word became man so that we could become members of God's family — God's people gathered together, the Church. And there is no question that it assigns a heightened role to the particular, or local, churches.

What is a "particular" church? Most commonly, the expression refers to a diocese (or similar ecclesial grouping) — a body of believers organized around their bishop in the celebration of the Eucharist. "Ecclesial communion, into which each individual is introduced by faith and by Baptism, has its root and center in the Blessed Eucharist. . . . The Eucharist is the creative force and source of *communion* among the members of the Church, precisely because it unites each one of them with Christ himself." The words are from a *Letter to the Bishops of the Catholic Church on Some Aspects of the Church Understood As Communion*, published in 1992 by the Congregation for the Doctrine of the Faith. Carrying the names of Cardinal Joseph Ratzinger, prefect of the congregation, and Archbishop Alberto Bovone, its secretary, it is a helpful statement of official thinking.

The letter says the Church of Christ *is* the universal Church, found in diverse "persons, groups, times and places." Among these are the local (or particular) churches — dioceses, for the most part — each entrusted to the care of a bishop, who is assisted by his priests. Implicitly, this is a rejection of the idea that Christ's Church exists first and foremost in the local churches (or, perhaps, in each individual congregation engaged in celebrating the Eucharist) and only secondarily and in a derivative way in the universal Church.

Rejection of any such notion as this is required for a right understanding of the idea that the universal Church is a "communion of churches." The document remarks that this sometimes is interpreted in such a way as to weaken "the concept of the unity of the Church at the visible and institutional level." History shows that when a particular church tries to become "self-sufficient," its internal unity suffers and it is at risk of losing its freedom — a thrust at the Gallican Church, the Church under Emperor Joseph II, and all the other churches, national and local, that in the centuries since Constantine have fallen under the sway of princes and potentates.

Quoting a 1987 address by Pope John Paul to the bishops of the United States, the letter makes the point that the universal Church is not just the sum total of particular churches or a federation comprised of these, as the rhetoric of the progressives sometimes suggests. "Ontologically and temporally," the universal Church comes before the particular churches: "ontologically," according to the Fathers, the universal Church "gives birth to" particular churches; "temporally," the Church of Pentecost, gathered around Mary and the apostles, and already speaking to all nations by the gift of tongues, preceded any local church.

The letter next makes the point that, in virtue of faith and Baptism, a member of the Church belongs to the *universal* Church, and this not "in a *mediate* way, *through* belonging to a particular Church, but in an *immediate* way." Of course, someone who belongs to the Church universal also belongs to a particular church, but these aren't two distinct, separate memberships; rather, this is "the same reality seen from different viewpoints." To be a member of the universal Church is to belong to the local churches everywhere, as is clear — above all — in the celebration of the Eucharist: a Catholic coming from one particular church is fully entitled to participate in the eucharistic celebration of another particular church on the opposite side of the planet, and to do so altogether naturally, without any special request or permission. For "whoever belongs to one particular Church belongs to all the Churches" by belonging to the one, undivided Church universal.

Unity or communion between particular churches and the universal Church is based not only on faith and Baptism, the document continues, but especially on the Eucharist and the episcopate. But having said that, it takes issue with the claim made by an exaggerated eucharistic ecclesiology, that "Church" comes into existence from the ground up, as it were, through the eucharistic celebration; on the contrary, a local community celebrating the Eucharist "achieves insertion into [Christ's] one and undivided Body," the Church as a whole.

Ecclesial unity also is grounded in the unity of bishops; and their unity depends on communion with Rome and its bishop, who — the document cites Vatican I and Vatican II — "as the successor of Peter, is a perpetual and visible source and foundation" of the unity of bishops and Church.

Finally, the letter makes the important point that papal primacy is not a principle standing outside and over against local churches; rather, it is an intrinsic part of their structure and being. Again it quotes John Paul II to the American bishops: "We must see the ministry of the Successor of Peter, not only as a 'global' service, reaching each particular Church from outside, as it were, but as belonging already to the essence of each particular Church from within." Petrine ministry doesn't impose itself on local churches in the way the federal government imposes its laws and regulations on states; it is a constitutive element of each particular church, shaping it from within and helping make it what it is.

The *Letter to the Bishops of the Catholic Church on Some Aspects of the Church Understood As Communion* says a number of other interesting and important things about *communio* ecclesiology. The points summarized here provide an interpretation of "communion" meant to protect the unity of the Church and the primacy of the Bishop of Rome against overemphasis on the "particular" and the "local."

An Inculturated Church

Two other general notions that frequently figure in this discussion are inculturation and subsidiarity. We shall look briefly at both.

Inculturation first. Adjustment to its environment obviously is necessary for the Church. In fact, today it may be more necessary than ever, considering how rapidly and profoundly the world is changing. If the Church is something like a living organism, as Catholics believe it to be, then it must adjust to changing circumstances to survive.

One argument for decentralization goes like this: The world of the twenty-first century is a very large and complex place. It's simply impossible to run everything from Rome; just as a practical matter, local decision-making is necessary. Archbishop Quinn recommends that the Church take a leaf from the book of multinational corporations, the United Nations, and the International Red Cross, and practice "directed autonomy," according to which people are encouraged to "do things their way," within boundaries prescribed by central authority.

People making this argument like to point to the fact that the center of gravity in the Church has shifted. It has "moved out of its European phase, evolving impressively into a world Church," says Cardinal Franz König, the retired archbishop of Vienna. "It is no longer Europe-centered: together with the Petrine office, it has discarded, or is in the process of discarding, its European mould. How to govern a Church of such diversity? We must decentralize."

At this point, the banner of inculturation is unfurled. And why not? At least in a general sense, "inculturation" is something every reasonable Catholic must applaud.

In its decree on missions, *Ad Gentes,* Vatican Council II identifies the positive heart of it when it says missionary activity "purges of evil associations those elements of truth and grace which are found among peoples and which are, as it were, a secret presence of God; and it restores them to Christ. . . . So whatever goodness is found in the minds and hearts of men, or in the particular customs and cultures of peoples, far from being lost is purified." Inculturation, as Vatican II explains it, enables the Church to incorporate and benefit from what is good in non-Christian cultures.

The Principle of Subsidiarity

Subsidiarity comes up often in arguments for decentralization, sometimes as a necessary tool for achieving it and sometimes as a desirable result of it. The ecclesiologist Patrick Granfield says that Cardinal Joseph Bernardin of Chicago, shortly before his death in 1996, remarked that subsidiarity was one of the biggest issues the next pope would have to face.

But there are at least two prior questions. The first is whether the principle of subsidiarity even applies to the Church; the second is whether, supposing it does, it applies in just the same way as in a non-ecclesial system, or whether there is something unique about subsidiarity in the Church.

Subsidiarity finds its classic statement as a principle of Catholic social teaching in Pope Pius XI's 1931 encyclical *Quadragesimo Anno* ("The Fortieth Year" — that is, since the publication of Leo XIII's groundbreaking social encyclical *Rerum Novarum*). Pope Pius wrote:

> Just as it is gravely wrong to take from individuals what they can accomplish by their own initiative and industry and give it to the community, so also it is an injustice and at the same time a grave evil and disturbance of right order to assign to a greater or higher association what lesser and subordinate organizations can do. For every social activity ought of its very nature to furnish help to the members of the body social, and never destroy them.

Archbishop Quinn argued at Oxford that subsidiarity definitely does apply to the Church. (Like some of the other matters he gave prominence at Oxford, subsidiarity gets surprisingly little attention in his book.) In support of this view, he cited talks by Pope Pius XII and Cardinal Giovanni Benelli,

Substitute Secretary of State under Pope Paul VI, a 1967 Synod vote to apply subsidiarity in the revision of the Code of Canon Law, and a passage in the preface to the 1983 Code saying subsidiarity should "all the more be applied in the Church" because of the Christ-given authority of bishops. Obviously, much more than that needs to be said to cover this topic adequately.

Cardinal König, adding his voice to those who argue for subsidiarity in the Church, nevertheless makes the point that it applies only to the Church's "visible structure," not its spiritual reality as a community of faith, hope, and love. As to the visible structure, he says, subsidiarity can be applied there "by analogy" — that is, in a way somewhat like and also somewhat unlike the way it applies to merely human societies. He also makes explicit the link between subsidiarity and collegiality:

> The human concept of subsidiarity does not prove that there has to be collegiality of bishops and pope, for that is a theological concept. But just as the human aspect of the Church can never be totally separated from the divine aspect, so collegiality is both human and divine. In that case subsidiarity helps us to get a clearer idea of what collegiality entails, showing us that each bishop has unrestricted responsibility for his own field of competence.

Unrestricted responsibility? That is hardly likely. Not even the pope has unrestricted responsibility and authority; rather, they are limited by the moral law and by the divinely given constitution of the Church. But if this is true of the pope, surely it is true of "each bishop." Still, the cardinal's basic point is clear: Subsidiarity provides useful guidance in working out the collegiality of bishops.

Items on the Agenda

Along with the various rationales advanced on behalf of the progressive program, the agenda of devolution includes a number of specific suggestions for change. These also range from the reasonable and moderate to the unreasonable and extreme.

1. General Councils

One suggestion often heard these days is for a new ecumenical council or similar collegial assembly to settle questions left unresolved by Vatican I and Vatican II and to adopt, or at least advance, the progressives' agenda of doctrinal and pastoral change. There is, however, no consensus on its nature and timing.

Paul Collins, the Australian theologian mentioned earlier, argues that a council definitely should be held; but, echoing a view others also express, he argues that it can only be a *general* council for the Western Church of the West, since no true *ecumenical* council is possible as long as the Church of Christ is divided into Catholic, Orthodox, Protestant, and Anglican.

This implies that there has been no ecumenical council since the eleventh-century split between East and West. And that, among other things, wipes off the books the dogmatic teachings of Trent, Vatican I, and Vatican II, including the dogmas of papal primacy and papal infallibility, reducing them — at most — to disciplinary regulations for the Western Church. A fairly radical suggestion.

As to site: "The next council should be held as far from Rome and the Vatican as possible in order to protect it from the machinations of the curia," says Father Collins.

Archbishop Quinn said at Oxford he would like to see a council held to start the third millennium. Thomas P. Rausch,

S.J., of Loyola Marymount University, Los Angeles, is sympathetic but warns against holding a council too soon, considering who would be there: "At the present time, over two-thirds of the Church's bishops have been appointed under the present pope's [John Paul II's] administration . . . a more systematic approach to ecclesial renewal should begin with a renewal of the episcopacy."

Thomas J. Reese, S.J., a social scientist and journalist who is editor of *America* magazine, wants an ecumenical council every twenty-five years, to "allow each generation of bishops to share their experiences, reflect on the state of the church, and act collegially." (Holding councils at frequent, regular intervals was an important part of the program of the Council of Constance and the Council of Basel in the high noon of Conciliarism.) On the very far left, the Constitution for the Church provides that national church councils every ten years shall elect the members of a general council to exercise supreme authority in the Church.

2. The Election of the Pope

How should popes be chosen? In the early centuries, the clergy and people of Rome made the choice, although frequently under pressure from the emperor or powerful Roman families pushing their candidates. The present system, according to which the electoral body is the College of Cardinals, evolved out of the practice of election by senior Roman clergy. As recently as 1996, it was confirmed by Pope John Paul. In a document revising the rules for papal elections, he gave two reasons why it is appropriate that the cardinals be the papal electors: because of their traditional link with the Bishop of Rome and because, coming from every continent, they express the universality of the Church and the universal outreach of Petrine ministry.

Suggestions for changing this system vary, but the general idea is to involve others besides — or in place of — cardinals. One objection to the latter is that they are too much the pope's men, handpicked by him and forming something like a papal cabinet or body of advisers. In fact, this role was reinforced by John Paul II's practice of calling the College of Cardinals together now and then in order to get their views — an advisory function progressives hold should have been reserved for the bishops' Synod.

Obviously, too, not a few cardinals are part of the Roman Curia and head Vatican congregations, hardly a recommendation in the progressives' eyes. Finally, it is said, papal election by the cardinals is not sufficiently in the spirit of episcopal collegiality, since the cardinals are a small, elite group within the body of bishops.

Who would join the cardinals, or take their place, in electing the pope? Bernard Häring says it would be a good idea to involve leading figures from "the Eastern churches and the traditional metropolitan churches in communion with Rome," together with the presidents of national conferences of bishops and "outstanding men and women." Thomas Reese recommends election by the ecumenical council or the Synod of Bishops. The Constitution for the Church wants a new pope chosen every ten years by the elected members of the worldwide general council; that body also would have authority to depose the pope before ten years were up if she or he wasn't doing the job to its satisfaction.

3. Upgrade the World Synod of Bishops
The Synod, an innovation of Vatican Council II, has been called potentially the council's most promising step toward finding an institutional embodiment of collegiality at the level of the universal Church. General assemblies of the Synod

now usually meet every three years; the rules also provide for other kinds of assemblies (regional, special) at the pope's pleasure.

If the Church today had no such institution as the world Synod of Bishops, it would be necessary to invent something like it. Yet bishops participating in these assemblies not infrequently come away less than pleased. There are complaints about cumbersome procedures, overly broad themes, manipulation by the Curia, secrecy, and the avoidance of topics deemed too sensitive to discuss. While sometimes overdone, these objections apparently are not without merit.

According to Archbishop Quinn, "Synods, if they were truly open and collegial events, could serve a very positive purpose. Synods, for example, could serve a purpose of preparing and refining the agenda for future ecumenical councils as well as dealing with short-term or emerging issues in the Church. . . . The likelihood is that truly open and collegial synods would enhance the moral authority of the Pope."

Instead of having a merely consultative role (making suggestions to the pope), it is suggested that the Synod be given deliberative power (authority to decide things, subject to papal approval); as a matter of fact, a pope *could* so empower the Synod even now. Involving it in the papal election, as some suggest, would ratchet up the power of the Synod even further.

4. Reform the Roman Curia

No item on the agenda for change evokes more impassioned rhetoric than the reform of the Roman Curia. This is the conglomerate of congregations, councils, and other offices and tribunals run by three thousand or so mostly clerical administrators and experts and lower-level staff who form the central administration of the Church and the papacy's administrative arm.

In the Vatican II years, the complaint often was heard

that the Curia was too Italian. Since then, the internationalization of upper-level staff and governing structures has largely been accomplished; the dicasteries, as they are called, operate under the oversight of standing bodies of mainly non-Roman cardinals and bishops, assisted by non-Roman experts. Now the complaint is that the non-Italians are as "Roman" in attitude and style as their Italian colleagues.

Lately, too, yet another complaint has surfaced: The Curia is doing what diocesan bishops should do. Partly this is said to involve giving orders to bishops and bishops' conferences, overriding their decisions, and the like. Diocesan bishops and others who go eyeball to eyeball with the Curia and lose sometimes strike a highly exasperated note. In a presentation prepared for delivery to the bishops of the United States shortly before his death in 1999, Cardinal Basil Hume of Westminster expressed annoyance at the "form and tone" of some curial letters, the manner and delay of episcopal appointments, failure to consult, and the way some theologians' writings were investigated.

Cardinal König writes that, while the Curia bears part of the pope's responsibility for the whole Church, it is just here that "the worldwide episcopal college should . . . take a hand" — and, for the most part, that isn't happening. Rather, "the curial authorities working in conjunction with the Pope have appropriated the tasks of the episcopal college." According to Archbishop Quinn, the Curia is at risk of seeing itself as a "tertium quid," a third force in the government of the Church, under the pope but over the bishops.

But complaints go even deeper than that. In fact, it looks very much as if some of the critics were using the Curia as a surrogate; instead of attacking the pope, they attack "Roman bureaucrats." They speak of taming the Curia in hope of taming the pope.

What sort of curial reform is needed? The most important step, from the reformers' point of view, would be to shift power from Rome somewhere else, especially to national conferences of bishops and diocesan chancery offices. As to restructuring the Curia, Thomas Reese offers several suggestions: Instead of using curial congregations and councils as decision-making bodies, convert them into oversight committees composed entirely of non-Roman members, such as the elected chairmen of the corresponding committees of national episcopal conferences; give these oversight committees the job of reviewing and critiquing staff "from the perspective of the local church"; make them part of the structure of the Synod.

Overall, Father Reese suggests that the Vatican become a "centralized clearinghouse, a forum for discussing ideas and programs coming from the local churches." Under such an arrangement, the pope would be "a facilitator of communication and a consensus builder rather than a monarch." Proposals like this appear to envisage the Holy See as a sort of home office administered by a weak CEO (the pope), wth policy set by a strong governing body (the general council, an augmented Synod of Bishops, or some other group representing national and local churches).

A recent biographer remarks that Pope John Paul himself is aware of the defects in the present curial system. Whatever might be said of some of the progressive proposals for correcting them, it is a long way from the pope as universal primate to the pope as universal facilitator.

5. Strengthen National Conferences of Bishops (and/or Comparable Structures)

Church history contains precursors and prototypes of today's national conferences of bishops. In the World War I years in the United States, the bishops set up an organization to coordinate the Catholic response to the national effort; it was called the National Catholic War Council. After the war, when some bishops sought to continue this body under the name National Catholic Welfare Council, others strenuously opposed the idea as a threat to their authority to govern their own dioceses. Rome was ready to shut down the organization entirely, but it relented in the face of assurances that it would not have authority over diocesan bishops and that it would be designated a "Conference" and not a "Council."

Headquartered in Washington, D.C., the NCWC served the bishops at the national level until replaced in the mid-1960s by twin organizations called the National Conference of Catholic Bishops and the United States Catholic Conference. (The latter was meant to evolve into a National Pastoral Council for the Church in the United States, but for various reasons that didn't happen.) At the time of this writing, NCCB and USCC are due to be replaced by a single organization, the United States Conference of Catholic Bishops, a step which will bring the U.S. setup in line with that in most other countries.

The modern episcopal conference is a creation of the Second Vatican Council. In its Decree on the Pastoral Office of Bishops in the Church, *Christus Dominus*, Vatican II described such a body as "a form of assembly in which the bishops of a certain country or region exercise their pastoral office jointly." The conference was to have decision-making authority, subject to approval by the Holy See, in certain defined areas (for example, liturgical norms). The Code of Canon Law and other documents add juridical specifics.

Most projects for taming the pope include giving bishops' conferences much greater authority than they now have to make decisions without seeking Rome's approval. But that points to an interesting question: Is the power of episcopal conferences to be enhanced not just at Rome's expense but at the expense of diocesan bishops?

For obvious reasons, this is not something people who favor more power for episcopal conferences say a lot about, lest some bishops get upset at the prospect of being ordered around by their own organization. The likelihood of that happening may be particularly great in the United States and other countries whose episcopal conferences are very large and sophisticated, with complex committee systems, hundreds of staff and advisers, multimillion-dollar annual budgets, and access to media that most diocesan bishops lack.

Some nevertheless do not shrink from drawing the conclusion. Klaus Schatz says the "real problem and task today" is not to strengthen individual bishops but to strengthen "supradiocesan structures" on the national or even "continental" scale. "Only those who think in categories of personal, monarchical, individual power can arrive at the conclusion, foreign to the ancient Church, that supradiocesan authorities can have no power over individual bishops unless it is given them by the pope," he says. Hermann Pottmeyer supplies a variation on this theme by calling for structures organized around patriarchs and patriarchates; according to this view, a "triadic" Church — local church with bishop, regional units with patriarchs, universal Church with pope — would realize the full implications of *communio* ecclesiology.

6. Selection of Bishops

While all pope-tamers speak of giving more power to local churches, things tend to become less clear beyond that point. Who is to be empowered by this empowering — diocesan bishops or somebody else? In the first instance, at least, the answer apparently is "somebody else," since changing the way bishops are chosen so as to give others more of a say is a big item on most agendas.

Thomas Reese says that, under the current system, "the pope is getting bishops who support his policies, but he is not getting bishops capable of winning over their people." Father Reese offers no evidence to support this statement, nor does he say whether it would be better for the pope to get bishops who *don't* support his policies but are good at winning people over, supposing both things simultaneously possible. The point is simply that the present system has to be changed.

For many centuries authority to name bishops was not claimed by the popes — not even by Gregory VII as he warred against Henry IV and lay investiture. And even though the papal claim was gradually asserted by St. Gregory's successors, it frequently was thwarted, especially in the centuries when Conciliarism and Gallicanism held sway. As late as 1829, the pope directly named only 94 bishops out of a worldwide total of 646 (now there are more than 4,000 bishops throughout the world). Only in the twentieth century, via the new Code of Canon Law and concordats negotiated with various countries, was the papal claim fully vindicated.

Proposals for changing the current system follow the familiar pattern, and range from the moderate to the extreme. The most moderate is simply to expand the consultation of priests and laity as part of the process. Another suggestion is to let priests and laity participate in drawing up the *terna* — the list of three candidates' names that the Vatican nuncio sends to the pope (the pope can, of course, choose somebody else).

Leftward down the spectrum lies the suggestion that the choice be made locally — by some representative group of clergy and laity — and sent to the pope for confirmation. This is not unlike the procedure mandated in the Civil Constitution of the Clergy in Revolutionary France in 1790. At the far end of the spectrum is the approach outlined in the Constitution of the Catholic Church:

> The Bishop shall be chosen by the Diocesan Council in accordance with the Diocesan Constitution, bearing in mind the appropriate regulations of the national and international communities, including consultation with and subsequent confirmation by the appropriate committees of the National Council and the General Council.

And what shall the bishop do?

> The Bishop shall serve as the leader of the Diocesan pastoral team. Within the policies set by the Diocesan Council, they [sic] bear the main responsibility for the worship, spiritual and moral instruction, and pastoral care dimensions of the Diocese, bearing in mind the principle of subsidiarity.

* * *

In his well-known book *Models of the Church*, published not long after Vatican II, Avery Dulles, S.J., wrote of the top-down ecclesiology dominating thinking for centuries up to that time. This was said to be a "pyramidal pattern in which all power is conceived as descending from the pope through the bishops and priests, while at the base the faithful people play a passive role and seem to have a lower position in the Church."

No doubt that was a true picture of some ecclesiological thinking before the council; it may even still exist here and there today. But, as this quick review of current thinking among Catholic progressives makes clear, other models of the Church now exist.

One envisages a decentralized but still essentially hierarchical system, with semiautonomous power centers — national conferences of bishops, patriarchates, perhaps some new form of regional or supranational structure — over against Rome. Another assumes a radical, bottom-up ecclesiology, with power flowing from the grass roots upward — a "people's church." There may be others.

The one thing today's pope-tamers agree on is that the present system has to go. But considering the wide range of conflicting alternatives they support, it seems all too likely that, if it did, the victors soon would fall to fighting among themselves over whose version of the Church would prevail.

A quarter of a century after *Models of the Church*, Father Dulles had this to say of suggestions advanced by Archbishop Quinn and other participants in the primacy debate:

> His proposals are not new. Many of them have been debated for generations. As for the principle of subsidiarity, Joseph Komonchak, whom Quinn cites as an authority, concludes that its application to the Church is "not yet ripe for solution." . . . The special charisms of the papal office, I believe, are especially important in the present era of globalization, when episcopal conferences are exerting unprecedented power. Great vigilance is needed to prevent multiple inculturation and the dispersion of authority from becoming divisive. Collegiality is essential, but it should not be understood in opposition to primacy, since the college of bishops cannot exist or function except with and under the primacy of Peter. Before demanding that the Synod of Bishops should have a deliberative vote one should carefully ponder who would be bound by its decrees. Does the whole Church really want to be legally bound by the majority vote of a

hasty gathering of selected bishops? The enthusiasm for the election of bishops that exists in some quarters might be tempered if Catholics had some experience of the party politics and electioneering that this would involve.

In other words: Better go slow on taming the pope.

CHAPTER FOUR

Evaluation of the Reform Agenda

As the Catholics in zeal and in union had a great advantage over the Protestants, so had they also an infinitely superior organisation. In truth, Protestantism, for aggressive purposes, had no organisation at all. The Reformed Churches were mere national Churches. . . . The operations of the Catholic Church, on the other hand, took in the whole world. Nobody at Lambeth or at Edinburgh troubled himself about what was doing in Poland or Bavaria. But Cracow and Munich were at Rome objects of as much interest as the purlieus of St. John Lateran.

Thomas Babington Macaulay
Ranke's History of the Popes

In the campaign to decentralize authority in the Church, the contemporary love affair with democracy often is visible. Everywhere today democracy is the all-but-universally approved system of governance — so much so that tyrants and demagogues pay it lip service and call their repressive regimes "democracies." In this climate it would be strange indeed if no one thought of applying democracy to the Church.

And why not? There is a lot to be said for democratizing the Catholic system. During the last two millennia, the Church has borrowed liberally from other forms of government, including those of imperial Rome, Renaissance Italy's city-states, and the European monarchies of the early modern era. Why not borrow from democracy now? It is said that the Church isn't a democracy. Yes, but neither is it an empire or a Renaissance city-state or a monarchy.

The arguments for democratization are basically two: the signs of the times require it, and it corresponds to fundamental elements of the Church. "The sources of Revelation clearly show that the church does indeed have some democratic factors," Archbishop Quinn said at Oxford. If some, why not more?

Whether it meant to do it or not, Vatican II lent support to democratization in speaking of the Church as the People of God. *Lumen Gentium*, the Dogmatic Constitution on the Church, calls attention to the fundamental equality — in dignity, mission, and rights — of all Christ's faithful, laity as much as clergy and religious. At the same time, nevertheless, it stresses the hierarchical structure of the Church, with diverse offices and functions, including those involved in exercising authority and obeying it.

Lumen Gentium is quite specific in speaking of both parts of this complex reality. First, diversity:

> The People of God is . . . made up of different ranks. This diversity among its members is either by reason of their duties — some exercise the sacred ministry for the good of their brethren — or it is due to their condition and manner of life.

And then equality:

> In the Church not everyone marches along the same path, yet all are called to sanctity and have obtained an equal privilege of faith through the justice of God (cf. 2 Pet. 1.1). Although by Christ's will some are established

as teachers, dispensers of the mysteries and pastors for the others, there remains, nevertheless, a true equality between all with regard to the dignity and to the activity which is common to all the faithful in the building up of the Body of Christ.

It is not unreasonable to think this calls for some degree of democracy in the forms and processes of Church life.

All the same, "People of God" is not a political or sociological idea, and democracy in the Church has serious, intrinsic limits. Insofar as "democracy" refers to a secular political system, it is not univocally applicable to the community of faith, which is a reality of a different order, partly human but also partly divine.

Take representation. Here is a fundamental principle of political democracy ("No taxation without representation"). In a democracy, people exercise the right to choose other people as their representatives in performing certain political tasks, especially decision-making. It sets the Christian tradition on its head to imagine that the pope or bishops "represent" the faithful in this sense; the pope and bishops do not represent the people but Christ. The relevant principles for exercising leadership in the Church are not representation but fidelity (to Christ and his Gospel) and accountability (to the people the leaders are meant to serve).

Central to accountability is the obligation to take responsibility for one's actions and render an account for them to the appropriate party or parties. Church documents leave no doubt that Church leaders are accountable to Christ, but it is not easy to find a clear statement of their accountability to the Catholic people. Perhaps the idea of stewardship offers a key to the source and limits of this.

Stewardship makes it clear that people are accountable

to those who entrust valuables to them for the use they make of what is entrusted. What do the people of the Church entrust to Church leaders? Obviously, money and temporal goods, including time and energy expended on Church projects; but also loyalty and trust itself. As stewards, the pastors of the Church have an obligation of accountability to their people for the money, time, effort, loyalty, and trust entrusted to them.

But accountability extends further. In a real and important sense, Catholics entrust their very souls to the leaders of the Church, inasmuch as they entrust their souls to Christ, who has chosen to act by means of the Church's leaders. This is the basis for the most important rights of the faithful: to sound doctrine proposed accessibly, to valid and licit sacraments readily available, to governance that directs cooperation toward the realizing of the kingdom. Speaking to the bishops of the United States in 1979, John Paul II said, "One of the greatest rights of the faithful is to receive the Word of God in its purity and integrity as guaranteed by the Magisterium of the universal Church." Does not the fact that the faithful have this right and others strongly suggest that they are entitled to vindicate their rights by insisting on the accountability of the pastors?

Ecclesial accountability should not be understood in juridical terms, as if it involved duties enforceable by law. The accountability of pastors is best understood on a familial model — it is something like the accountability of a good father to his loved ones. And that, clearly, is not reducible to "representation."

Consider another central principle of political democracy, majority rule. Majority rule makes good sense in secular society — provided the community's life is based on sound moral principles and norms and is organized around a sound understanding of the common good. (But democracy is corrupted if this consensus breaks down and majority rule is used to legitimatize violations of moral truth over the objections of a conscientiously dissenting minority. John Paul II speaks of this abuse in his 1995 encyclical on human life, *Evangelium Vitae*.)

Majority rule cannot be a central principle of Church governance. The most important reason, attested to by abundant scriptural evidence as well as by definitive teaching, is that this is not what Jesus had in mind. Instead, he gave supreme authority to teach and govern the Church to Peter and his successors, and to the apostles and theirs.

There are other reasons, too, among them the fact that questions of revealed truth cannot be settled by majority vote. Yes, someone might object that the Holy Spirit guides the *sensus fidelium* — the consensus of the faithful — and could as easily do that via a system of voting, or even opinion polling, as in any other way. But even if one granted that, it would remain the case that the *sensus fidelium* isn't an independent principle for settling doctrinal questions, but is subject to the discernment and judgment of the Magisterium, the teaching authority of the Church residing in the pope and bishops. No doubt popes and bishops act reasonably in taking the *sensus* into consideration, but in no way are they bound by it. Failure to grasp that, says Terence L. Nichols, an American theologian, is at the root of distorted "egalitarian" thinking.

Moreover, as another American theologian, Germain Grisez, points out, the Church's common good — divine-human communion — is entirely a gift of God. As such, it is not open to the conventional means-ends analysis (what do we need to do to achieve it?) involved in decision-making by majority rule in a secular democracy. Divine-human communion is not something we can decide and act to achieve; either God gives it or we don't have it, and our duty in its regard is not to be efficient in gaining it but faithful in preserving it and zealous in making it available to others.

Still, majority rule and other democratic processes might be appropriate — today, might even be highly desirable — in some areas of Church life. Among them are matters of temporal administration — raising and spending money, opening and closing institutions, inaugurating new programs (or ending old ones) for carrying on fundamental activities like evangelization and catechesis, even many personnel decisions.

These thoughts about democracy apply to proposals for changing the exercise of papal primacy. In each instance two basic questions must be answered at the start: Is a "democratic" way of doing things possible in this case, given the nature and structure of the Church and the reality of primacy, as the dogma has been defined; and, if possible, is it a good idea? Hans Urs von Balthasar remarks that some proposals for a democratized Church floated after Vatican Council II would have turned the papacy into "a kind of church presidency." Some of today's pope-tamers apparently would welcome that; yet even now most Catholics would probably demur, seeing it in conflict with the constitution of the Church willed by Christ.

Principles of Decentralization

Now let us turn to some of the principles invoked by decentralizers: collegiality, subsidiarity, inculturation, and the rights of particular, or local, churches. There is something to be said for and against each.

Collegiality

Early in the twentieth century, when Ultramontanism was in the saddle, a writer on the papacy argued that it presented "no difficulty" for Catholics to be governed by two rulers — the pope and their own bishop — and cited the case of soldiers commanded simultaneously by a general and a regimental commander to illustrate the point. Aside from the fact that many people now would look askance at the military metaphor, the analogy breaks down when a military chain of command is compared with the relationship of primacy and collegiality.

In the army, a general gives orders to a regimental commander, and the latter is obliged to carry them out. Today, hardly anybody would say that is how pope and bishops are related. Vatican Council II declares: "Whilst loyally respecting the primacy and preeminence of their head, [bishops] exercise their own proper authority for the good of their faithful, indeed even for the good of the whole Church."

If the model of a military chain of command won't do, what will? That's harder to say. "The dispute over collegiality is not a battle between Pope and bishops over sharing power in the Church," says Cardinal Ratzinger; but he admits it can "very easily degenerate into this kind of fight." A delicate, hard-to-find balance must be struck if that is not to happen.

The Bishop of Rome is head of the College of Bishops but also a member of the college; while standing above the college from one point of view, he does not stand outside it or apart. "The Bishop of Rome is a member of the 'College,' and the Bishops are his brothers in the ministry," Pope John Paul says in *Ut Unum Sint*. As we have seen, even Vatican I's *Pastor Aeternus* declares:

> This power of the Supreme Pontiff [primacy of jurisdiction] is so far from interfering with that power of ordinary and immediate episcopal jurisdiction by which the bishops . . . individually feed and rule the individual flocks assigned to them, that the same (power) is asserted, confirmed, and vindicated by the supreme and universal shepherd [the pope].

111

Vatican I goes on to quote Pope St. Gregory the Great to this effect. And even though the language of shepherds and flocks may not be everybody's favorite way of speaking of bishops and the Catholic people today, the point is clear: Bishops, in the words of *Lumen Gentium*, are not mere "vicars of the Roman pontiff" but "vicars and legates of Christ."

At the same time, it would be a serious mistake to suppose that the pope receives his authority from the college or is merely the bishop designated to serve as its presiding officer and mouthpiece, and executor of its decisions, while being subject, as radical Conciliarism would have it, to removal from office at the pleasure of the college. Nor is the pope limited to teaching and governing the Church only in a formally collegial manner, after consulting the bishops so as to reflect their consensus. Nor does collegiality mean the pope can't arrange the affairs of a particular church and immediately and directly exercise pastoral authority over its bishop, clergy, and people. No doubt it is desirable that popes generally teach and govern in consultation with their brother bishops — as in fact they often have done — and keep out of the affairs of local churches except when obliged to intervene for the good of souls (this also has sometimes been the case). But, whatever institutional and procedural expressions it may have now or in the future, collegiality should not be understood to mean the pope has less than supreme authority everywhere in the Church, which he can exercise according to his own conscientious judgment.

Collegiality implies a role for bishops, individually and together, in relation to the universal Church. But the bishops cannot act collegially — the episcopal college can't function — apart from their head, the pope. The bishops' collegial role has been expressed especially in and through ecumenical councils, convened, or at least recognized, by the pope and confirmed by him. Today, it also is manifested, at least analogously, in the Synod of Bishops, whose assemblies express the "collegial spirit," exhibit "affective collegiality," and the like.

It is open to question whether episcopal collegiality should routinely be in play at the level of the universal Church. Cardinal Ratzinger holds that bishops generally best serve the Church as a whole by doing a good job pastoring the particular churches entrusted to them.

> Individual bishops share in the government of the universal Church not by being represented in some central organ but by leading as shepherds their particular Churches which together form and carry in themselves the whole Church . . . whose health and right government does not simply depend on some central authority but on the right living of the individual cells both in themselves and with relation to the whole. It is in governing the particular Church that the bishops share in governing the universal Church.

In this view, putting too much stress on the bishops' role in the central government would reflect a fundamental misjudgment: "It is the expression of a centralism which the Second Vatican Council in fact wanted to overcome."

Subsidiarity

Many of those who want to enhance collegiality see the principle of subsidiarity as a necessary means to that. Hermann Pottmeyer lists subsidiarity as one of three principles to guide the development of "structures of communion" (the others are collegiality and cooperation — understood as a single principle — and catholicity). Structures concretely expressing subsidiarity will make it possible for "decisions that do not threaten the unity and communion of the universal church to be made within limited regions of the church," he writes.

A statement prefatory to the proposed Constitution for the Catholic Church says bluntly: "The principal level or forum of Christian life takes place at the community or parish level, and therefore, through the notion of subsidiarity, it is at that local level where most of the decision-making should take place." This reflects a typical mistake of people — conservatives as well as liberals — who think of the Church according to a political model. In fact, most decision-making in the Church does not, and should not, occur at the parish level, any more than at the level of the diocese or the national bishops' conference or the Vatican. Most decision-making, as well as the actual living of Christian life, takes place at the level of individuals and families.

Provided one understands that fundamental fact about decision-making in the Church and sets aside political models that situate its primary *locus* elsewhere than the individual and the family, it is clear that subsidiarity *does* apply. Let us look at what that means.

The Church is one body with many members, each with its own proper gifts and functions. The "members" include a variety of units — dioceses, religious orders, parishes, a multitude of particular communities and groups, families, individuals. In each case, the larger community should help those within it fulfill their proper functions, not take them over.

The great difference between the Church and political society is not in the meaning, relevance, or application of subsidiarity. It lies in the common good of the whole, the proper functions of each group and individual, and the ways of supplying help.

Bear in mind again that the Church's common good is divine-human communion, which primarily depends on God's

114

activity — on grace — not on what we do. The whole point of ecclesial life is to receive, enjoy, cherish, and pass on to others this God-given gift and other divine gifts that contribute to its development and eventual perfect fulfillment in the kingdom of God.

By contrast, in political society realization of the common good depends on the actions of leaders and citizens, and the actions are based on their decisions. The common good itself is not ultimately fulfilling for the society's members but only instrumental to their fulfillment — a means to an end; that fulfillment is something they must pursue in and through other associations, beginning with the Church.

Talk about subsidiarity in the Church often confuses matters by mistakenly assuming that ecclesial leadership has essentially the same job as leadership in a political society — namely, decision-making that leads to action. But from the most important point of view, Church leaders and members have nothing very important to decide and nothing very important to argue about. The leaders' job is to identify what has been given by God, safeguard it, and preside over the cooperative activities of the members in receiving, enjoying, and cherishing it, and making it available to others. "Decision-making" as such is of very secondary importance in the Church, and the argument about subsidiarity in Church decision-making of similarly limited importance.

Instead, what is of great importance are the building up and the preservation of ecclesial unity. The Petrine ministry — the office and action of the pope — is first and foremost a service to that unity. Pope John Paul links primacy and unity in a striking passage in *Ut Unum Sint*.

> The mission of the Bishop of Rome within the College of all the Pastors consists precisely in "keeping

watch" (*episkopein*), like a sentinel, so that, through the efforts of the Pastors, the true voice of Christ the Shepherd may be heard in all the particular Churches. In this way, in each of the particular Churches entrusted to those Pastors, the *una, sancta, catholica et apostolica ecclesia* [one, holy, catholic, and apostolic Church] is made present. All the Churches are in full and visible communion, because all the Pastors are in communion with Peter and therefore united in Christ.

Calling the Bishop of Rome "the first servant of unity," he says:

> This primacy is exercised on various levels, including vigilance over the handing down of the Word, the celebration of the liturgy and the sacraments, the Church's mission, discipline and the Christian life. It is the responsibility of the Successor of Peter to recall the requirements of the common good of the Church. . . . He has the duty to admonish, to caution and to declare at times that this or that opinion being circulated is irreconcilable with the unity of faith. When circumstances require it, he speaks in the name of all the Pastors in communion with him. He can also — under very specific conditions clearly laid down by the First Vatican Council — declare *ex cathedra* that a certain doctrine belongs to the deposit of faith. By thus bearing witness to the truth, he serves unity.

"All this, however, must always be done in communion," he immediately adds.

The Church's unity in regard to its common good does not rule out subsidiarity regarding other matters. But unity in what pertains to the common good is vastly more important — it's of the essence of the Church. If it can be maintained unimpaired at the same time subsidiarity is observed in the rather limited area of decisions that need to be made in the Church, then subsidiarity should be respected. But if subsidiarity conflicts with unity in what pertains to the common good, it must be excluded.

Inculturation

Jesus' fundamental instruction to his disciples was to spread the Gospel, and when that is done, the Gospel becomes intertwined in human affairs and acquires cultural accretions. Christians attempting to spread the Gospel in new cultural settings where it has not yet been received must strive to set aside accretions acquired in a different culture and relate the good news to the culture of its new hearers. This, in very general terms, is inculturation.

The "Chinese rites" controversy of the seventeenth and eighteenth centuries often is cited as a horror story supposedly illustrating the bad things that happen when the Church fails to inculturate. This long-running argument pitted Jesuit missionaries against others in the China mission over how far to go in accepting Chinese customs and beliefs in the practice of Christianity by Chinese converts. Particularly at issue were certain aspects of Confucianism, the use of ancient names for God, and, especially, ancestor worship. The Jesuits held that in allowing their converts to retain these things they were merely letting the Chinese be Christians without giving up their cultural identity. The critics argued that the practices in question were of doubtful orthodoxy or simply unorthodox. Both sides still have their defenders.

Pope Clement XI banned the Chinese rites in 1715. This decision was reaffirmed by Benedict XIV a quarter-century later. In the twentieth century, Pope Pius XI reconsidered the whole matter in light of changed circumstances and allowed some things that — perhaps rightly — had not been allowed two hundred years before.

Despite the complex, controverted facts of the Chinese rites controversy, today's decentralizers like to speak of the episode simply as an avoidable setback for evangelization that should not be repeated. Here, they say, is an illustration of the evils of Roman decision-making. In the twenty-first century, the Church's need to be inculturated in non-European settings is even more pressing than it was three or four centuries ago.

The only reasonable reply to this is: Yes, but. . . . Yes, the Catholic Church in Africa or Asia or Latin America — or the United States, for that matter — shouldn't be burdened with European trappings that make it alien in the eyes of local people. But no, the Church in Africa or Asia — or even the U.S. — mustn't give up essential elements of Catholic faith.

What are we to make, for example, of appeals on behalf of "Asian theology," "Latin American theology," and the like? The experience of Catholics in Asia, Latin America, and other parts of the world offers relevant material and helpful insights for the process of theologizing. But is that all these expressions imply? What did the Jesuit provincials of Asia actually have in mind when they said in a statement in 1999: "We . . . need to be mindful of the legitimate pluralism in theology within the unity of faith and of the subsidiarity in decision making in a church that is also a communion of local churches." Obviously, no one is going to admit to a hankering for *illegitimate* pluralism — but what do generalities like this really mean?

One of the concerns about Asian theology, for instance, is the possibility that faith in the uniqueness of redemption in and through Jesus Christ might be undermined by exaggerating the salvific potential of Eastern religions. As for African inculturation, the suggestion has sometimes been made that this might require accepting clerical concubinage (out of respect for African ideas about maleness) or polygamy or living-together as part of an extended betrothal rite (out of respect for African marriage customs).

Are there principles to help us decide what is acceptable in this matter and what is not? The distinction between inculturation, on the one hand, and adaptation and assimilation, on the other, may help.

Inculturation involves transforming what is good in a non-Christian culture: it is, one writer remarks, "the Christianization, the redemption, the baptism, as it were, of non-Christian language, symbolism, art, poetry, and other literature." Adaptation (a theological process) and assimilation (psychological and sociological processes) also can be good and helpful. But they are bad from a Christian point of view when they are "an expression of nationalism" or involve "the adoption of symbols and customs generally known to belong essentially to the non- or anti-Christian sphere [which] is a road leading back to paganism."

The Pontifical Council for Culture calls inculturation "inseparable" from evangelization. Nevertheless, in *Towards a Pastoral Approach to Culture*, a document published in 1999, this Vatican body also noted problems. The most serious in some non-Western parts of the world was said to be syncretism: trying to cobble together a composite religion from various sources — a little Christianity here, a little Buddhism there, a little New Age Gnosticism someplace else. "In our times, religious ignorance is feeding the different forms of syncretism between ancient and now extinct cults, new religious movements and the Catholic faith," the Council for Culture said.

For the secularized cultures of the first world, it added,

the most serious problem is secularism. This was said to involve a systematic undermining of religious faith leading to "a serious cultural and spiritual crisis" of individuals and groups. Obviously that applies to a considerable body of culturally assimilated American Catholics, who, having uncritically plunged into the social mainstream, have interiorized attitudes and practices fundamentally in conflict with their own religious tradition, from treating Sunday Mass and the other sacraments as optional to supporting the "right to choose" abortion mentality.

Globalization adds a new dimension to the inculturation debate. It has profound cultural implications as well as economic ones. While it may be premature to speak of a global culture, the signs of cultural homogenization — McDonald's in Moscow, Toyota and Sony in Cleveland — are everywhere.

This raises an interesting question for advocates of a more inculturated Church: With the tide of globalization running strongly the other way, isn't it counter-intuitive (at least) to put so much emphasis on indigenizing Catholicism? Granted, the time has long passed when it seemed the right thing to do to link Christian missionary efforts to European colonialism. But if we are heading toward a world culture or some approximation thereof, how much sense does it make to press the Church to become more African or Asian — or even more American — than it is? As for Catholics in the United States and other countries of the secularized West, should they not be cultivating a tad more counter-culturalism instead?

In any case, merely demonizing globalization would be a mindless response to a process that appears certain to go forward, thanks to new communications technology. The energies of concerned Catholics might better be spent trying to ensure that, as globalization proceeds, priority is given to persons over corporate profits in sharing its economic benefits. As other institutions and groups organize themselves for this new transnational and transcultural world, the Catholic Church cannot responsibly walk away from it. And, as Cardinal Francis George of Chicago points out, one advantage enjoyed by the Church in seeking to evangelize in an era of globalization is precisely its catholicity:

> As a church extended throughout the entire world, the Catholic Church is a transnational institution which brings special resources to a globalized world. In an age when transnational institutions (such as the NGOs [nongovernmental organizations]) can render a special service to mankind which no single nation can do, the Church has networks of communication to build solidarity among nations and throughout the human community. The challenge . . . is to use the network we already have even more effectively.

This is not an argument against inculturation. It is an argument against understanding it in a narrow and parochial way, and then attempting to make it an absolute ecclesiological principle.

Something else needs to be said at this point. Throughout much of the twentieth century, a variety of totalitarian regimes labored to separate local Catholics from Rome by fostering national churches or their equivalent. Although this was from one point of view a coerced, contemporary version of Gallicanism, in certain respects it also resembled an abuse of inculturation.

The Nazi ideologue Alfred Rosenberg, a bitter foe of Catholicism, complained that Rome sought to create a "nationless world Church" instead of accepting the kind of tame local churches that suited him and his Nazi colleagues. In Yugoslavia after World War II, the communist dictator Tito pressured Cardinal Alojzije Stepinac to head a breakaway Croatian church separated from Rome. When Stepinac refused, he was subjected to a farce trial and sentenced to sixteen years at hard labor. (After serving time in a labor camp, the cardinal was transferred to a rectory where he remained under house arrest until his death in 1960.)

In Vietnam, where the situation of Catholics in fact is said to be improving, a 1999 government decree, replacing a similar document issued in 1991, requires the prime minister's approval for the appointment of bishops. "Directions" coming to the country's bishops "from abroad" are to pass through the bureau of religious affairs. Seminaries must be approved by the ministry of education. Provincial committees must give the green light for the ordination, assignment, or transfer of priests. For religious activities over and above those registered in an "annual plan of activities" to take place outside a church, a special permit is needed.

The Republic of China affords an especially painful example of this oppressive mentality at work. The trials of the Catholic Church under a half-century of communist rule there are well known. In the 1950s, says one longtime China observer, the government attempted to "force Catholics to break all allegiance to the Pope" and accept an "Anglican settlement" — that is, a national church; this effort enjoyed partial success through the creation of a government-approved Catholic "patriotic" association. Even so, a substantial body of Catholics remained loyal to Rome and constituted an underground Catholic Church.

Following a relaxation of religious policy around 1980, the Chinese authorities moved to a Gallican arrangement in place of the Anglican one. "Now, in a Gallican situation," writes Audrey Donnithorne, formerly of the Contemporary China Centre at the Australian National University, "no one is compelled to renounce an article of faith. But . . . loyal Catholics have to exercise ingenuity as well as prudence in maintaining links with the universal Church."

And as this is written, early in 2000, the patriotic association has lately ordained five more government-backed bishops without papal approval. A Vatican spokesman expressed "the surprise and disappointment of the Holy See" at the move, which was interpreted as part of a new government crackdown on Catholics loyal to Rome as well as upon the autonomy of Chinese religious bodies in general.

Undoubtedly the Church needs inculturation, but adaptation and assimilation are a different story, especially when they are linked to religious syncretism or involve absorption into a hostile secular culture. As for coerced conformity of the sort that the authorities in China and other places have tried — and go on trying — to impose, it is totally unacceptable.

The Particular Churches

One of the most significant Catholic ecclesiological developments of recent decades has been the reemergence of a *communio* ecclesiology emphasizing particular, or local, churches. The *Letter to the Bishops of the Catholic Church on Some Aspects of the Church Understood As Communion*, the 1992 document of the Congregation for the Doctrine of the Faith that was discussed earlier, gives a helpful overview.

It may be the most important insight of this way of thinking that the Church does not exist *only* in the universal Church or *only* in the particular church but simultaneously, and necessarily, in both. As Joseph Komonchak says, "The church is not *catholic* if it is not particular, that is, *local*; but the particular, or local, is not the church unless it is *catholic* at every level."

But rough spots in the relationship remain to be worked out. It isn't easy to keep in focus an entity — the Church of

Christ — at one and the same time present and real at both the universal and local levels. One naturally supposes either that "church" is *really* present in the local church and somewhat less present in the universal Church (which then takes on an abstract, notional character), or else that the *real* Church is the universal Church, of which particular churches are, as it were, branch offices.

As that suggests, there is a real danger of overemphasizing one dimension or the other: if universal, then not really local; if local, then not truly universal. Pushed to an extreme, the second mistake points to the conclusion that what is called the "universal Church" is only a federation of local communities — particular churches — which alone deserve to be called "church" in a full and real sense.

This is not acceptable. Michael Buckley remarks, "The universal Church is not the sum of the local churches. The local church is the Church universal as it is present and operative and actualized in this particular place and culture. If it is not the universal Church, it is not the Church at all; it is a sect. These churches are not bound by federation, but by the common sharing of those principles that constitute and generate the Church."

But that also is obscure. How can the local church be the universal Church? The analogy of the body sheds some light. A living body is one thing, with parts. As one thing, it has one identity and one name: "John's body." Its parts also have identities, but these are subsidiary, as it were; the common identity of all is the identity of the body as a whole. The parts do not give the body its identity — the body gives their common identity to the parts: John's arm, John's leg, John's ear; what is common to each is "John's."

Perhaps the Church is something like that. Particular churches have their particular identities, but these are of a subsidiary kind. The identity common to all and making them one is their identity as Christ's Church. Particular churches do not give the Church of Christ its identity; rather, the universal Church of Christ supplies the common identity of the particular churches. And just as John is not the collection of his body parts, so the universal Church is not simply a collection of particular churches; but, at the same time, just as there is no John without at least his vital body parts, so there is no universal Church without the Church at Rome and particular churches in communion with it.

Trying to use political and sociological models to illuminate the relationship of universal to local in the Church ends in confusion. But something even worse than confusion results when a eucharistic ecclesiology drawn from Orthodox sources is pressed too far. Here is Orthodox writer Philip Sherrard: "Where Christ is manifest in the Eucharist, there is the Catholic Church. And as Christ is manifest in each local church in which the Eucharist is celebrated, each local church is itself *the* Catholic Church." What this seems to overlook is that the eucharistic community not only is worldwide but, even more, is the entire gathering of those baptized in Christ and united with him in the self-offering he continues to make in heaven. The universal Church is present in, though not reducible to, the particular eucharistic community when it celebrates the Eucharist, for each celebration unites *this* congregation with the one, unending heavenly liturgy. Moreover, besides destroying the unity of the universal Church, the way of thinking expressed by Sherrard appears to leave little or no room in principle for such other constitutive elements of the Church as evangelization, catechesis, and serving human need.

These days, nevertheless, thinking resembling that of Philip Sherrard and other Orthodox writers often turns up in the ecclesiological musings of Catholics bent on devolution.

Its appeal would appear to lie in the fact it provides a rationale for pushing decentralization about as far as it can go.

But this way of thinking about the particular churches also has another non-Catholic source — Protestant congregationalism. Just as some Orthodox think it is the Eucharist that, virtually alone, brings the Church into being, so the same role is played for some Protestants by the preaching of the word. But since the word is preached in and to a local congregation, it is essentially there — in the local congregation — that Christ's Church can be found. The Savoy Declaration, a congregationalist manifesto of 1658, draws the necessary conclusion: "Each of these particular churches is the Church in the full sense of the term and is not subject to any outside jurisdiction." Although historical congregationalism has a synodal structure of church governance, the supracongregational synods have no real authority over local congregations.

If unchecked, a reductionist emphasis on principles like subsidiarity and the primacy of the particular church can only lead in time to some "Catholic" version of congregationalism. Of course, today's reformers do not usually say that, and many probably don't entirely grasp the fact. Yet the principles they one-sidedly espouse lack any more fundamental principle to halt the slide into congregationalism.

Indeed, some progressives do seem to know that. Paul Collins, for one: "The local community is the foundation. . . . The local community is the primary locus of decision making." And the sponsors of the Constitution for the Catholic Church: "The principal level or forum of Christian life takes place at community or parish level."

Finally, though, the centrifugal dynamic of this kind of ecclesiology moves beyond even the local congregation, to the isolated individual and his or her private, interior religious experience.

In a paper given at a symposium on Archbishop Quinn's Oxford address, American theologian Wendy M. Wright remarked: "To a present day Catholic participating in a Quaker-inspired clearness committee, a practice which affirms that the Spirit dwells with egalitarian elegance in the hearts of all the gathered listeners, it may begin to seem quaintly anachronistic that the present pope [John Paul II] appears to be clutching Peter's keys closer and closer to his chest so that genuine discernment in the Roman Church has become reduced to listening, not to the heart, not to the wider and deeper tradition, not to the voices of trusted advisors, not even to scripture . . . but to the voice of Rome alone."

On one level, this is just an ugly caricature of John Paul II; but, on another, it is an accurate expression of the mentality of those Catholics for whom "discernment" is an essentially solipsistic exercise in consulting their personal preferences and those of like-minded friends. The underlying principle of congregationalism, which progressive Catholics have adopted, is that the individual's relationship to God (for example, through personal conscience) is of overriding importance, while the coming-together of individuals in associations (churches) is merely secondary — a way of having the experience of community. From this point of view, the associations that are nearer to hand — local congregations — naturally seem more important than any larger network formed by such local groups (the universal Church).

The Framework of Vatican I and Vatican II

Someone trying to be faithful to the Catholic tradition is obliged to evaluate proposals for changing the papal primacy's manner of exercise by the standard of the First and Second Vatican Councils. Not all would-be reformers are open to that.

Here and there one finds Catholics echoing the Orthodox contention that no real ecumenical council has been held since at least the Catholic-Orthodox split in the eleventh century — and none can be held as long as the Churches are divided. Trent, Vatican I, Vatican II, and the rest? Not ecumenical councils at all, just councils of the West. That wipes off the books the inconvenient dogmatic definitions of papal primacy and infallibility. Neither the Magisterium nor serious Catholic theologians seem likely to accept the idea.

"As always," von Balthasar remarks, "the only path after definition is that of an integration into a larger, all-embracing whole." Serious-minded proponents of decentralization like Hermann Pottmeyer and Klaus Schatz agree. The former rejects the idea that "a reform of the papacy is possible only if one relativizes or even denies the binding character" of the two dogmas. The latter rejects out of hand the idea that Vatican I might one day simply be set aside as "erroneous"; doctrinal development, if any, must be in continuity with what it taught.

Father Schatz nevertheless argues that the teaching of Vatican I does not entirely rule out some of the ideas associated with Conciliarism and Gallicanism and some new forms and institutions in their spirit. Just as what Vatican I taught about primacy and infallibility cannot be rejected, he writes, so "neither are the contrary positions 'rejected' once for all. The episcopalist and Gallican lines of thought also endure as a stimulus to the Church and as witnesses to a broad current of tradition that has to be taken seriously."

Is this true? Possibly, provided the emphasis is placed on generic concepts like "a stimulus to the Church" and "a broad current of tradition" that needs to be taken seriously; but not if the statement means that the Church, reversing gears, now must embrace historical expressions of Conciliarist and Gallican thinking like the decrees of Constance and Basel declaring a council superior to a pope, or the Four Articles Concerning

Ecclesiastical Power adopted by the French clergy congress of 1682. These expressions of virulent Conciliarism and Gallicanism *are* ruled out by the solemn definitions of Vatican Council I, solemnly confirmed by Vatican Council II.

So are quite a few other ideas advanced in the name of taming the pope. For example, that the Bishop of Rome can *only* teach and govern the Church in a formally collegial manner — together with the College of Bishops (the desirability of his consulting the bishops is a very different matter); or that autonomous national churches, free to accept what the pope says or ignore it, are compatible with the essential oneness of the universal Church. Whatever Catholics of the fifteenth or seventeenth century may have thought about these matters, they are not open questions or acceptable options any more. They have been settled by Vatican I's definitive teaching about papal primacy.

Similarly, papal primacy is not reducible to a primacy of honor; nor is the pope merely the Church's CEO, responsible for carrying out the will of a council or synod or some other body. Councils may be held from time to time in the future, with great impact; the role of the Synod of Bishops could, and quite possibly should, be rethought and expanded (more of that below); new forms of collegial assembly and process may emerge. But the pope's supreme and unimpeded authority to govern and teach the whole Church, universal and particular, must still be acknowledged; it may not be so hedged about with conditions and procedural requirements that, in practice, the pontiff could only act in formal collaboration with some other body.

Similar caution, even skepticism, is required regarding the claim that popes over the centuries sometimes have taught and legislated as Patriarchs of the Western Church rather than pastors of the universal Church.

It could be that they have. The distinction, or something like it, can perhaps be glimpsed in the fact that John Paul II promulgated a new Code of Canon Law for the Western Church in 1983, and then, in 1991, promulgated another, separate code for the Oriental (Eastern) Church. In the first instance, someone might argue, he acted as Patriarch of the West, in the second as universal pastor.

But even if that is so, it does not follow that popes routinely have acted on the basis of any such distinction between their "Western" and "universal" roles. On the contrary, in teaching and legislating, they commonly seem to have had it in mind to teach and legislate for the whole Church everywhere. Although this is a serious question that merits scholarly investigation, in the present, relatively undeveloped state of knowledge it would be irresponsible to try to use it to adjust papal authority downward — for instance, as part of a poorly thought-out project of drawing closer to the Orthodox.

Specific Proposals Evaluated

Against this background, we can take a look at some specific proposals for change.

The Synod of Bishops

The suggestion is that, in one way or another, the Synod's role be significantly enlarged. Currently its main job is giving advice and suggestions to the pope on themes or topics of his choosing; it is "consultative" only. It is said the Synod should become "deliberative" instead — it should have a role in decision-making. Canon law already allows this, at the pope's discretion.

Other suggestions are that the Synod participate in electing the pope, that its membership be constituted in some other, more representative way than now (some participants elected by national conferences of bishops, some appointed by the pope, and some — the heads of Vatican departments — essentially *ex officio*), that it have more leeway in choosing its topics, conducting its discussions, and making public statements of its own.

All of these changes are possible, in the sense that none would violate any doctrine. Some would be useful, especially those that focus on allowing the Synod to function freely, whether in a consultative or deliberative role. But, for reasons to be explained below, involving the Synod in the election of the pope could cause serious problems. (A different suggestion for expanding its role will be examined in the next chapter.)

The Ecumenical Council

An ecumenical council is a full, formal, solemn expression of episcopal collegiality at work at the level of the universal Church. Here the bishops of the world teach and legislate for the whole Church, in union with and under the headship of the head of the college, the pope.

As with the Synod of Bishops, there are various suggestions for changing how the council is organized and what it does. Must only bishops take part? No — nonbishops participated in earlier times, and it might be a good idea to resume that practice, although finding a fair and efficient way of choosing nonepiscopal participants, especially laity, and defining their role would not be easy. Probably, too, there is merit in the suggestion that representatives of non-Catholic Christian churches have an expanded role at future councils, beyond their observer status at Vatican II; but that role also would need careful defining. It would not be possible for any participants but Catholic bishops to have an actual vote; but certainly there are ways of playing a meaningful role in such a gathering without voting.

Routinely holding ecumenical councils at regular intervals — every ten years or every twenty-five years — as some progressives now urge, would *not* be a good idea. In fact, this would be the backdoor return of the radical Conciliarism definitively rejected by Vatican Council I.

Ordinarily, ecumenical councils best serve the Church when they are held to address specific questions and deal with specific problems that require the attention of the supreme authority in the Church. But holding a council every quarter-century or so would turn the assembly into a kind of parliament, convening regularly to legislate and set policy whether new laws and policies were needed or not. Moreover, with the development of new communications technology, it will be increasingly possible for the bishops of the world to exchange ideas and information and deliberate together, without the need to haul them out of their dioceses periodically and bring them together in unwieldy assemblies of several thousand. Some of those pushing for regularly scheduled councils apparently want to set the council over the pope — to reduce the role of pope and Curia in practice to carrying out the decisions of one assembly and making preparations for the next.

The Roman Curia

No doubt the Curia does need reform; it always has and always will. The Roman Curia is a bureaucracy, and although it includes many holy, devoted, and talented servants of the Church, it also has a bureaucracy's faults, not least a tendency to claim unwarranted authority for itself. *Curia semper reformanda*, one might say.

Insofar as reform would mean shifting power from the Curia to other ecclesiastical bureaucracies, however, it is an idea of extremely doubtful merit. Taking power from one bureaucracy and giving it to another does nothing to deal with the faults of bureaucracies in general and in this case might magnify them, if their newly acquired power went to the heads of a multitude of Church bureaucrats in bishops' conferences around the world.

What some people urging reform of the Roman Curia seem to mean is: Give more power to the staffs of bishops' conferences. Having spent some years working for one of these, I can report that, just like the Roman Curia and the curias that inhabit chancery offices in countless dioceses, national Church bureaucracies have the same bureaucratic faults, including casual and ingenuous arrogance, loss of touch with the grassroots, and eagerness to acquire power for themselves.

A longtime staff member of one large conference tells me that when he came on board, senior colleagues explained that the role of the organization's committees — defined in the bylaws as policy-setting — was to offer suggestions to the staff.

By all means reform the Roman Curia. Reform them all!

Conferences of Bishops

Bishops' conferences are more than their bureaucracies, though; they also are the bishops themselves. When proponents of devolution urge that episcopal conferences be given more authority, they generally mean empowering national hierarchies, although sometimes other supranational or subnational episcopal groupings also are envisaged.

It could be done. Canon law specifies what bishops' conferences can decide without reference to Rome, and expanding their authority is certainly possible. Some bishops think their conferences are kept on too short a leash by Rome and get too much second-guessing from the Curia. Being closer to the scene, they say, they have a better feel for pastoral realities; besides, collegiality and subsidiarity require this step.

Bishops' conferences are evolving entities. For thirty

years, there was a lively argument about whether statements by these bodies had magisterial authority. In 1998, to the surprise of some, John Paul II said they did, provided the statements were adopted unanimously by the bishops or, having gotten a two-thirds vote, were then approved by the Holy See. Despite knee-jerk complaints by some progressives that this was overly restrictive, it was a major concession. There could be more.

Here, too, prudence suggests a go-slow approach. The obvious danger in going too far down this particular road is a relapse into Gallicanism. Avery Dulles cautions: "The exercise of a totally independent magisterium by the conferences could lead to divisions in the church and to a species of ecclesiastical nationalism detrimental to catholicity." If bishops' conferences are to have a role in teaching and governing, then, just like individual bishops, they must teach and govern in communion with other bishops and the Bishop of Rome. New norms and procedures to ensure that would be essential.

Proposals for giving more power to bishops' conferences also ignore certain political facts of life. Empowering these bodies to make decisions binding on diocesan bishops (beyond the few already permitted by existing canon law) is something many of the latter have no intention of allowing, since it clashes with their conviction that, although a bishop is answerable to the pope, he is not, ultimately, answerable to his peers for how he runs his diocese. Better than anyone else, they also understand that, as in any other political institution, so also in an episcopal conference, not all bishops are equal. Some individuals and cliques generally run the show, while the rest have only limited say. In light of that, some bishops would be pleased if conferences of bishops had less power, not more.

Cardinal Godfried Danneels of Mechelen-Brussels, Belgium, a prominent European churchman who is no conservative, expresses a widely shared skepticism about giving bishops' conferences more power. They do have a role to play, he conceded in an interview. "But I would not give them too much importance because I am always fearful that they will reduce the Church to a national church. . . . I come down on the side of the autonomy of each diocese. . . . I'm against intermediaries with the universal Church. . . . I would not want, for example, the bishops' conference to say to the bishops: We have voted in the majority and you, the bishop of this diocese, must do what we have agreed. . . . [T]he fixed points are the universal Church and the local church. The intermediate bodies are instruments of assistance."

Having said this, however, one must also say that various other steps pertaining to bishops do deserve consideration. These include breaking up overly large archdioceses and dioceses into smaller, more manageable units, and entrusting some matters (for example, liturgical translations — a matter of controversy in the United States and other countries at this time — and the preparation of model catechetical materials) to language groupings working under the supervision of the supreme authority. The issue isn't power and who shall wield it; it is involving bishops to a greater extent than now in transdiocesan and transnational affairs where they can play an appropriate role.

Papal Elections

Certainly the present system for electing the pope could be changed. Quite possibly it should. There is no intrinsic reason why the cardinals, and nobody else, must elect the pope. But insofar as proposals for change aim to make the electors more representative, it is necessary to ask: Representative of whom and what?

Time and again in centuries past, emperors and Catholic princes interfered in papal elections, imposing candidates, vetoing candidates they didn't like, extracting promises from candidates as the price of not blocking them. The last such intervention, as we saw earlier, was in the conclave of 1903, when Emperor Franz Joseph of Austria vetoed Cardinal Mariano Rampolla, Secretary of State under Pope Leo XIII. Word of the imperial veto was brought to the conclave by the cardinal-archbishop of Cracow; Pope John Paul's 1996 rules strictly forbid any cardinal to repeat that performance.

Emperors and Catholic princes do not veto candidates for the papacy today. But it would be naïve to suppose that somehow rules out the possibility of external pressure from other sources in the future. Making the papal electors more "representative" than they are would open the door to that.

The pressure could come from ecclesiastical sources as well as secular ones. It is easy to imagine electors being seduced by overtures to promote the special interests of their national churches or episcopal conferences (or their governments). To be sure, the present system of choosing popes can be abused; but making the electors more representative of somebody or something back home would seriously jeopardize the integrity of the process.

Besides having presidents of bishops' conferences serve as papal electors, it is sometimes suggested that the Synod of Bishops or the ecumenical council play this role. Along with being another backdoor route to Conciliarism, that also is highly unrealistic. Besides inviting pressure from interest groups, turning the election of the pope over to two hundred (in the case of the Synod) or four thousand (in the council's case) jet-lagged bishops largely unknown to one another would be an invitation to manipulation by a small, well-focused group with an agenda. If the present system of election by the cardinals is to be changed, the change should be an improvement, not a setting for disaster.

The Selection of Bishops

Changes also are possible in the way bishops are chosen. But it misrepresents history to suggest that giving local churches more say would mark a return to a golden age when local communities of faith freely selected their own leaders. There may have been some times and places where this more or less was the case, but it seems to have been the exception, not the rule. And except for Christianity's first three centuries or so — when the new religion often was a persecuted, underground movement — no such idyllic state of affairs existed for long.

On the contrary. During much of the last millennium and a half, the choice of bishops often was dictated by secular rulers. Bernard Häring says papal appointment of bishops is a carryover to the Church from "an era of political centralism and authoritarianism"; but the papacy's struggle to assert control over the process wasn't a Roman power grab but an attempt to free the Church from the grip of the state.

It was slow work. Even in the early twentieth century, the governments in Spain, Portugal, Bavaria, and several Latin American countries chose candidates for the episcopate whom they presented for confirmation to the Holy See; so did the Austrian government, except for certain dioceses, and so had the governments of France and some other Latin American countries done until not long before. In several Austrian dioceses, as well as in Switzerland, Prussia, and some German states, cathedral chapters elected bishops — but the electors couldn't choose candidates of whom the civil authorities disapproved. In Italy, the government insisted that bishops named by the pope have the king's approval before taking office. (Catholicism in the United States was blessed by being spared government interference in the selection of bishops. Franklin Roosevelt's behind-the-scenes campaigning in 1939 for one candidate for archbishop of Chicago and against another —

Archbishop Samuel Stritch of Milwaukee, who got the job — was an exception.)

The 1917 Code of Canon Law for the Western Church reserved the choice of bishops to the pope. This policy was implemented in the following years through a series of concordats between the Holy See and governments of countries where this was not already the practice. Even so, in some places the civil authorities continued to have a voice in this matter until quite recently.

Now, of course, it appears that Rome finally has gotten its way — the selection of bishops rests with the pope. Bishops themselves have some input, mainly by compiling and updating lists of suitable candidates on a provincial basis; but when the time comes to appoint a bishop, the pope appoints him, usually acting on the advice of the papal nuncio as it is filtered through the Congregation for Bishops.

Granted the desirability of concentrating this authority in the papacy at a time when governments routinely intervened, someone might say, the time and the need for that have passed. Encroachment by the state is no longer a problem; the particular churches should be allowed to choose their bishops, or at least should have a much larger say.

But the unhappy situation in countries like China and Vietnam makes it clear that government efforts to dominate the Church and control the choice of bishops are not everywhere a thing of the past. Before trying to push the pope into the background, Western Catholics without experience of persecution by their governments would do well to ponder the plight of their brothers and sisters in countries with totalitarian regimes.

Papal selection of bishops also is an important safeguard against potential abuses like electioneering, pressures from interest groups in and out of the Church, and the likelihood that a diocesan process would fall under the de facto control of a dominant clergy faction and its lay allies. Proposals for moving in this direction must be very realistic about the risks; and changes, if any, should be made cautiously and evaluated carefully at every stage. As a first step, it might be possible to devise a workable system whereby local Catholics, including laypeople, would participate in compiling the *terna* — the list of candidates' names — that goes to Rome. For the unity of the universal Church and the good of the local churches, however, diocesan bishops should continue to be designated by the Bishop of Rome.

'The Primacy of the Successor of Peter . . .'

In 1998 Cardinal Ratzinger and Archbishop Tarcisio Bertone, prefect and secretary of the Congregation for the Doctrine of the Faith, published a paper called *The Primacy of the Successor of Peter in the Mystery of the Church*. It is helpful to take a look at it as we round out this overview of proposals for change.

The Primacy of the Successor of Peter in the Mystery of the Church begins by noting the "exceptional importance" of this subject for ecumenical reasons, especially after the encyclical *Ut Unum Sint*; it was this that led the Congregation for the Doctrine of the Faith to organize its symposium on papal primacy in 1996. The present document is meant to recall "essential points" of Catholic doctrine about primacy — "Christ's great gift to the Church" for its service to unity, which has "often defended the freedom of Bishops and the particular Churches against the interference of political authorities."

Primacy's origin, purpose, and nature, starting with Peter ("the ministry of unity entrusted to Peter belongs to the permanent structure of Christ's Church. . . . The Catholic Church teaches, as a doctrine of faith, that the Bishop of Rome is the

Successor of Peter in his primatial service") are reviewed, and primatial service is said to be above all a service of unity. The nature of papal primacy was taught clearly and definitively by Vatican Council I; Vatican II "reaffirmed and completed" that teaching, especially by its doctrine regarding the particular churches and episcopal collegiality.

All members of the College of Bishops have some responsibility for the well-being of all the churches and the universal Church. But "in the case of the Bishop of Rome . . . the *sollicitudo omnium Ecclesiarum* acquires particular force because it is combined with the *full and supreme power* in the Church: a truly episcopal power, not only supreme, full and universal, but also immediate, over all pastors and other faithful. The ministry of Peter's Successor, therefore, is not a service that reaches each Church from outside, but is inscribed in the heart of each particular Church."

In its essence and its exercise, the papacy is not like governing offices in human societies — it is "not an office of coordination or management" — nor can papal primacy "be reduced to a *primacy of honor*, or be conceived as a political monarchy." The Roman Pontiff is *servus servorum Dei*. As such, he does not make "arbitrary decisions," but is "spokesman for the will of the Lord." Thus the exercise of primacy has "limits set by divine law and by the Church's divine, inviolable constitution." Peter's successor is "the rock which guarantees a rigorous fidelity to the Word of God against arbitrariness and conformism."

Through the exercise of primacy, the pope serves unity in handing on the word, in the celebration of the liturgy and sacraments, in discipline, and in the norms of Christian life. In all these areas, everyone in the Church, including bishops, owes obedience to the pope, who also is "guarantor of the legitimate diversity" found in the Churches of the East and the West.

Given its episcopal character, primacy is first expressed

in transmitting the word; therefore it includes responsibility for evangelization. Responsibility for transmitting the word also includes a supreme and universal teaching office, whose exercise in some cases involves infallibility.

Along with his teaching role, the pope has a right to "perform acts of ecclesiastical governance" as unity of faith and communion require — for example, giving the mandate for the ordination of new bishops and requiring that they make a profession of faith; issuing laws for the whole Church and establishing "pastoral structures" for particular churches; giving binding force to the decisions of councils; approving supradiocesan religious institutes, etc. "Since the power of the primacy is supreme, there is no authority to which the Roman Pontiff must juridically answer for his exercise of the gift." But this does not mean he has "absolute power"; rather, "listening to what the Churches are saying is . . . an earmark of the ministry of unity, a consequence also of the unity of the Episcopal Body and of the *sensus fidei* of the entire People of God."

The nature of papal primacy is "immutable," but it has "historically been expressed in different forms of exercise," and at any given time its "concrete contents" will depend on the needs of the Church. These contents cannot be determined simply by identifying "the least number of functions exercised historically." Rather:

> The fact that a particular task has been carried out by the primacy in a certain era does not mean *by itself* that this task should necessarily be reserved always to the Roman Pontiff; and, vice versa, the *mere* fact that a particular role was not previously exercised by the Pope does not warrant the conclusion that this role could not in some way be exercised in the future as a competence of the primacy.

Whether something belongs to the primacy is a matter for discernment by the pope, in dialogue with his brother bishops and in light of the Church's needs. But "only the Pope (or the Pope with an Ecumenical Council) has . . . the authority and the competence to say the last word."

Cardinal Ratzinger and Archbishop Bertone add that this review of Church doctrine on primacy is useful in avoiding "the continual possibility of relapsing into biased and one-sided positions already rejected by the Church in the past (Febronianism, Gallicanism, ultramontanism, conciliarism, etc.)." They close with an expression of hope for Christian unity: "We are all invited to trust in the Holy Spirit, to trust in Christ, by trusting Peter."

Primacy and Unity

However the exercise of papal primacy might change in the future, the pope's role as a principle of ecclesial unity must be kept clearly in view, defended, and upheld. The pope is not *the* principle of unity; the Holy Spirit is. But the pope is *a* principle of unity, and an indispensable one. He does not perform this service through a symbolic primacy of honor, but by authoritative teaching and governing. Yet even though he is not subject to any other authority in the Church, the pope is totally subordinate to Christ, and the answer to the question "Who will guard the guardian?" is in this case: "The Holy Spirit." Someone who is not satisfied with that answer does not exhibit Catholic faith.

The papal service of unity is something constitutive of the Church. Other ways of exercising papal primacy besides those of the past and present can be imagined; better ways could always be found. But the primacy of the Bishop of Rome may not be undermined or impeded for the sake of taming the pope.

In its paper on the Church as communion, the Congregation for the Doctrine of the Faith sketched a version of *communio* ecclesiology that does not subvert papal primacy or weaken the unity of the universal Church; but the debate goes on. Already, though, it is clear that, while particular churches and local congregations should have a more prominent place in Catholic thinking, this cannot be at the expense of the unity of the universal Church and the service to unity rendered by papal primacy — a service involving the routine exercise of real jurisdictional and teaching authority.

People who argue for a return to the model of the early centuries sometimes say the faith of the Roman Church and its bishop then served mainly as a passive norm of orthodoxy; the pope intervened in the affairs of other churches only when asked to settle disputes that could not be settled locally. But even supposing that were an acceptable arrangement for the Church today — a doubtful supposition, considering the rapidity with which news of local disputes and abuses, and the harm, now are spread by modern media — it would be essential that Rome truly *function* in this way. That would require practical working structures and mechanisms of governance to ensure that it did.

For the sake of the particular churches themselves, the promoting of their interests cannot be used as an excuse to exclude papal jurisdiction. Petrine ministry is not extrinsic to a local church; as John Paul II says, it is "a requirement of the [particular] church's very constitution, and not . . . something added on from without for historical, sociological or practical reasons."

Newman remarked that if one reflects upon the "absolute need" that the Church has for papal primacy, one naturally expects to find it becoming fully visible at just the appropriate time, while the consequences of abandoning this principle likewise are all too apparent.

A political body cannot exist without government, and the larger is the body the more concentrated must the government be. If the whole of Christendom is to form one Kingdom, one head is essential; at least this is the experience of eighteen hundred years. As the Church grew into form, so did the power of the Pope develop; and wherever the Pope has been renounced, decay and division have been the consequence.

That is as true now as when Newman said it in 1845. It will remain true in the future. As the local churches need the vicars of Christ called bishops, so they and the universal Church of Christ cannot do without the Vicar of Christ called pope.

CHAPTER FIVE

The Once and Future Papacy

But the unique institution has survived; and at this hour of decision at which we now live it is meet and right that all men and women in the Western World who "have been baptized into Christ" as "heirs according to the promise," and with us all the Gentiles who have become "partakers of the promise" and "fellow heirs of the same body" through the adoption of our Western way of life, should call upon the Vicar of Christ to vindicate his tremendous title.

Arnold J. Toynbee
A Study of History

Sorting out the strands of the papal primacy debate, one comes to a conclusion that, although reasonably obvious, nevertheless is sometimes overlooked: A strong papacy and a strong episcopate both are necessary. And both are necessary not just for the sake of the Church but also, as Arnold Toynbee's plea above suggests, for the sake of the world.

Start with the Church. Michael Buckley argues that primacy and episcopate can be understood as "relations," and especially as related to each other. If that is so, then any treatment of the Church lacking a healthy appreciation of both cannot help but be incomplete. From this perspective, it is not enough just to say that the First Vatican Council dealt with the doctrine of the papacy but, forced to break off prematurely, did not get around to bishops. Rather, in saying so much about the pope and so little about bishops, the story told by Vatican I, while true, could only be part of the entire story. It remained for Vatican Council II to pursue the "rediscovery of the Church" that Cardinal Ratzinger reminds us had begun even earlier, by speaking about episcopal collegiality.

Although Vatican II did a surprisingly good job at this, it left a number of questions unanswered, and they have remained so up to now. That is not all bad. Trying to answer too many questions too soon can be a mistake; and many important questions in the Church are best illuminated by the lived experience of the People of God. Still, these particular questions do need answers, at least provisional ones, for the sake of the Church's harmony and good order. We need a working consensus here and now on primacy and collegiality, while remaining open to further insights in the future.

Surely everyone can agree that the papacy and the episcopate best serve the Church when both are strong and functioning as they ought to be, with the balance not tipped too far in either direction, as it was by radical Conciliarism on the one hand and extreme Ultramontanism on the other. Granted the hierarchical structuring implied by the very idea of primacy, bishops nevertheless are vicars of Christ, not branch managers of a multinational organization with its CEO in Rome; while the Bishop of Rome is *the* Vicar of Christ, holder of the Keys and supreme pastor and teacher of the entire Church, universal and particular, and not just a figurehead symbol of unity. As a practical matter, strains in the relationship of universal and particular are visible today not just at the level of popes and bishops but also at the grassroots. This is most apparent in the case of pope-tamers whose hearts are set on weakening the papacy; but it is hardly less visible in the case of conservative Catholics who seem to regard pa-

pal authority — or even the authority of a Roman congregation — as a useful club to belabor their bishops and pastors
on matters, from liturgy to doctrine, that are important to them.
Sometimes, of course, such people also can be seen shrug-
ging off what the pope says when it does not suit them —
papal teaching on the duties of rich nations to poor and John
Paul II's teaching against capital punishment are cases in point
— but that's another story.

In any case, all that being as it may, the lesson for our
present discussion is clear. At the same time that we relearn a
proper appreciation for the particular churches — as well as
for ecclesial groupings at the national and regional levels —
the universal character of the Church must be preserved. "I am
against a rigid definition of national churches," says Cardinal
Godfried Danneels. "The Church must remain universal; it must
feel universal. That's where its freedom comes from."

Here, too, the papacy's transnational governing and teaching initiatives are essential. History repeatedly has shown that
religious bodies too closely tied to a national or ethnic identity
are at risk of becoming captives of the temporal powers. On
this point, Hans Urs von Balthasar cites the testimony of the
Russian religious philosopher and advocate of Catholic-Orthodox reunion Vladimir Soloviev. Pointing to the "continu-
ous, humiliating repression" of the Russian and Greek Churches
by political powers-that-be, he observes: "Anyone who will
not have Peter as leader automatically becomes prey to the secular powers and to nationalism."

Many years ago G. K. Chesterton, a man of large and
generous spirit, confessed that he was "ashamed" at discover-
ing that, although prepared to accept a black cardinal, he was
not ready for a black pope. Black cardinals have become com-
monplace since Chesterton's day. If, at the time this is written,
we have not quite reached the point of having a black pope, at

least the universality of the Church of Christ holds out the possibility of that happening better than anything else could do. In fact, humanly speaking, much of the strength of Christ's Church lies precisely in the fact that, although present and active nationally and locally, it is *not* a national or local church. Petrine ministry in the universal Church is an important part of what is needed to keep it that way, together with courageous leadership of the particular churches by their bishops.

In Service to the World

The well-being of secular society, the "world," also requires a strong papacy and a strong episcopate. Of course, their service is not always greatly appreciated; on the whole, the world might prefer to ignore popes and bishops, denigrate or dominate them, even eliminate them. Still, their service — a true service, not a return to the clerical domination of politics and culture to which churchmen aspired in the late Middle Ages — is essential in an era that, even more than Toynbee's, is an "hour of decision," a time of cultural crisis.

So large and all-encompassing is this global crisis that its outlines can be only dimly perceived. Part of it revolves around radical skepticism, the fundamental postmodern doubt about whether there is any such thing as objective truth or whether, supposing there is, that truth can be known. Afflicting many people today, Christians among them, this systematic doubt is at the heart of the "nihilism" of which John Paul II spoke in his 1998 encyclical, *Fides et Ratio* ("Faith and Reason").

> Perspectives on life and the world, often of a scientific temper, have so proliferated that we face an increasing fragmentation of knowledge. This makes the search for meaning difficult and often fruitless. Indeed, still more dramatically, in this maelstrom of data and facts in which

we live and which seems to comprise the very fabric of life, many people wonder whether it still makes sense to ask about meaning. The array of theories which vie to give an answer, and the different ways of viewing and interpreting the world and human life, serve only to aggravate this radical doubt.

The epistemological question — can truth be known? — is central to the conflict between secularism and theism, and between the former's disregard of fundamental rights of persons and communities and the latter's witness to them.

The indispensable contribution that Catholics and other Christians are called on to make to resolving this crisis requires of them at least two things. One is that they resist assimilation into a secular culture permeated by radical skepticism. The other is that they carry on a vigorous program of evangelization. Both call for strong ecclesial leadership — leaders who can articulate the cultural identity of the Church community and give decisive direction to its coordinated action. This is a large part of the task of a Petrine ministry corresponding to the needs of the present day; it also is an important part of the ministry of bishops, working not at cross purposes but in harmony, which they can only do consistently by working in concert under the direction of the pope.

Popes of the last two centuries have been strong leaders. John Paul II stands squarely in this line, and not all Catholics have welcomed this.

Some, for instance, have been visibly embarrassed by the Vatican's strong opposition to abortion, contraception, and coercive population control on the occasion of several United Nations population conferences, and have made it clear they would prefer to bow to the secular consensus rather than buck the tide. But the challenge to fundamental human values so evident on such occasions creates a clear need for energetic exercises of Petrine ministry, and these deserve the bishops' support. Where this is lacking, episcopal authority suffers a great deal more than the pope's, while the Church as a whole is in danger of being co-opted by the state. Starting in the very early centuries of Christianity, as Newman pointed out, "again and again would the civil power, humanly speaking, have taken captive and corrupted each portion of Christendom in turn, but for its union with the rest, and the noble championship of the Supreme Pontiff." It seems improbable that in the twenty-first century Caesar somehow has lost his age-old impulse to control and corrupt.

Individually and collectively, bishops, alongside the Bishop of Rome, need to play a larger leadership role than they have sometimes done lately in confronting the challenges of the anti-Christian secularized culture abroad in the West today. Bishops are neither the pope's local representatives nor his rivals for power. They are leaders — pastors — of the Church in their own right, with a duty to teach, sanctify, and govern the faithful in union with the pope and one another.

Complaints about Roman overcentralization and excessive intervention by the Curia in local affairs have a basis in fact. But they also reflect episcopal omissions — failures to take the initiative and lead. In the last three decades, American Catholicism has suffered an embarrassingly large number of cases in which egregious problems, from publicly dissenting theologians holding positions of trust to notorious abuses in matters of liturgy and pastoral practice, have been ignored, even though they were nationally or even internationally notorious as a result of media publicity. In some of these cases, Rome finally stepped in; and then the cry "Roman interference!" not uncommonly was raised, even though the fundamental problem was that local authorities had not done their job. (One way bishops might "do their job," incidentally, would be for the bishops of a province or region to join in persuading an erring brother either to mend his ways or resign.) One reason for such diffidence on the part of local Church authorities may be a certain lack of intellectual formation leading to an exaggerated tendency to defer to "experts" — in which case the obvious solution would seem to be more and better intellectual preparation, for all seminarians but especially for those whose gifts indicate that they might one day occupy important leadership positions in the Church.

Over on the far right, some extremists would be pleased if the pope routinely exercised close top-down control at all levels in the Church, including dioceses. Their mirror images on the left want it just the other way — de facto independence for national churches (or local churches — the progressives aren't always clear), with authority flowing upward from the grassroots through representative electoral processes. Most Catholics who think about these things would probably prefer a reasonable middle ground.

But finding it will mean making some practical changes. What might these be?

That question deserves careful thought and discussion by many people. The following ideas are offered in hopes of encouraging that.

Service and Authority in the Church

Basic truths about the Church and ecclesial leadership have to be kept in mind when possible changes in the structures of papal primacy and episcopal collegiality are being considered. One such truth is that the essential function of Church leadership is, in von Balthasar's words, "unceasingly to focus attention on . . . transcendence and even to represent it." The reality of the Church and of ecclesial leadership is misrepresented when thought of simply in "immanent" — that is, sociological or political — terms.

Certainly the Church has a human, sociological dimension, whose neglect leads to misrepresentations of a different sort, in particular, the dualistic notion of a disembodied "spiritual" Church, separate from, and intolerably burdened by, the "institutional" Church of mere human beings and their relationships and interests. But it is the reductionism of viewing the Church only in sociological terms that underlies the "anti-Petrine attitude" (the expression is von Balthasar's) found even among members of the Church from early times until now. Thinking this way about the Church turns legitimate questions concerning the relationship between papal primacy and episcopal collegiality, the universal Church and the particular churches, the Roman Curia and bishops' conferences, into political issues and power struggles.

Church leadership has a duty to serve the Church's common good. But, as Germain Grisez notes, this common good is divine-human communion. It is a divine gift, not a human achievement, realized above all in the celebration of the Eucharist, and is a beginning here and now of the *communio* of the heavenly kingdom. The central and indispensable ministry of ecclesial leaders is to safeguard this gift. And that requires the exercise of authority in teaching and governing.

Just at this point, though, another dualistic temptation not uncommonly emerges. It is the temptation to dichotomize service and authority, and suggest that in the Church service is a good thing but authority is not.

Authority can be misused in the Church quite as much as anywhere else; history is full of such cases. But authority is by no means in and of itself the same thing as authoritarianism. While the latter is an abuse, authority as such is a good and necessary property of responsible leadership. As von Balthasar points out, it is futile to try to avoid the word — and the reality — of authority, substituting "service" instead. For "the People of God benefit from a service only when 'authority' is effectively present: for authentic proclamation, for government, for administering the sacraments."

Church leaders are obliged to have care for both the universal Church and the particular churches. The pope and the other bishops share this responsibility. But the pope has a universal primacy that the other bishops do not have. The others can govern and teach the universal Church only when acting as a collegial body in union with the pope, and never apart from him; the pope can teach and govern the Church either in collaboration with the episcopal college or on his own.

Grisez notes that Jesus had good reasons for structuring Church leadership as he did, and specifically for entrusting supreme authority *both* to one member of the college and yet *also* to the college when it includes and acts together with that one member. (I am drawing here on Dr. Grisez's thinking on this subject as it is set forth in a privately circulated preliminary outline of volume four of his comprehensive work on moral theology, *The Way of the Lord Jesus*. Since he is anxious that the tentative character of this outline be respected, I shall not quote directly from it.)

Among the reasons for giving primacy to one member of the college were: the necessary requirements for organizing and leading the bishops in cooperating for the good of the Church as a whole and doing so as more than a collection of pastors of particular churches; the physical impossibility of the whole college acting in some circumstances and the great difficulty of its doing so in others; the need to legitimize, through the pope's participation, actions taken on behalf of the whole Church by only part of the college.

But there also were good reasons for Jesus to give supreme authority to the college, as long as it includes its head. These include increasing the credibility of its members' witness to the faith by making it clear they are not mere subordinates of the pope; and making the Church as a whole a more recognizable sign and more adequate instrument of divine-human communion. Each bishop, including the pope, stands toward his particular church *in persona Christi*, as Jesus stands toward the Church as a whole; so each must be joined to the others in a *collegium* whose members can stand together *in persona Christi* toward the whole Church. If, however, other bishops were merely subordinates of the pope, then only he would stand *in persona Christi* to the whole Church; and that would obscure the *in persona Christi* relationship of the other bishops to their particular churches, as well as the subordination of the pope — along with the rest of the clergy — to the service of Jesus and the faithful.

The responsibilities of the supreme authority of the Church — pope and bishops together — extend to four matters. These are, in Grisez's formulation: the ministry of unity; the evangelization of nonbelievers; certain services to the particular churches (for example, establishing general plans of action, providing liturgical regulations, texts, and translations, supplying guidelines and materials for evangelization and catechesis, establishing and regulating national episcopal conferences); and a mixed bag of other services that the supreme authority is best equipped to provide (electing the pope, appointing bishops, establishing dioceses, canonizations, indulgences, and so forth).

The ministry of unity stands first among these responsibilities. It includes preventing and overcoming disagreements among bishops on essential matters of faith; preventing and healing schisms; trying to prevent practices that might invalidate the Eucharist and other sacraments; and promoting reconciliation with separated Christian groups that do not include validly ordained bishops. (The bishops of certain other groups, such as the Orthodox, are validly ordained and so already belong to the episcopal college, even though they are not in communion with their Catholic brothers, including the Bishop of Rome; thus their churches have an entirely different relationship to the Catholic Church from that of other separated Christian groups. To speak precisely, they cannot be "reconciled" with the Catholic Church in the same sense as groups without bishops; rather, it is a case of restoring communion.)

Finally, it is essential to respect the principle of papal freedom of which von Balthasar speaks: To perform his ministry of spiritual liberation on behalf of the People of God, the pope himself must be free.

> Peter really needs the freedom that has had to be fought for down the centuries in the face of Conciliarism, Protestantism, Gallicanism, Jansenism, Josephism, Febronianism, etc. All these placed his office in shackles in order to . . . give authoritative freedom to themselves. Whereas, if the primacy was taken seriously, there seemed to be a danger of inviting the bearer of this office to use this authority irrespective of *communio* and *collegium*, the conditions demanded by these movements actually *accomplished* a break in *communio* and *collegium* by restricting the exercise of the primatial ministry and denying the primate his liberty to perform his . . . liberation.

Von Balthasar adds that these historical factors made the First Vatican Council necessary, "no matter how 'inappropriate' or incomprehensible its definition regarding the primacy may seem to the spirit of our age." Vatican I "responded to a critical situation in the Church" arising from the French Revolution, the collapse of the *ancien régime*, and the emergence of the aggressive, anticlerical laicism and secularism that followed.

Next, a few practical suggestions.

Teaching and Traveling

Popes should publish fewer teaching documents than they have been accustomed to do lately, and bishops should publish more. As matters stand, and have stood for a long time, the teaching office of the bishops is at risk of being overshadowed by the sheer quantity of teaching from Rome. The teaching authority of pope and bishops alike would be enhanced by striking a better balance in this matter.

The point is not that popes should never teach or issue teaching documents. On the contrary, this very often is appropriate and necessary. Starting in the late nineteenth century with Leo XIII and continuing until now, however, the number of papal documents — encyclicals, apostolic exhortations, allocutions, statements, and messages of all sorts — has enormously increased.

Take encyclicals. Over a period of fifteen years, Pope Gregory XVI (1831-1846) published nine. Pope Pius IX published thirty-seven in thirty-two years (1846-1878). But Leo XIII issued eighty-six in twenty-five years (1878-1903). While Pope Leo holds the record up to now, popes of the twentieth century produced a steady stream of encyclicals — to say nothing of other teaching documents (and to say nothing, either, of the many documents from the Roman Curia that somehow carried the weight of pontifical authority). Although Pope John Paul II's thirteen encyclicals in his first nineteen years were a relatively modest number compared with some, they generally were much longer than Leo XIII's had been and were accompanied by a vast outpouring of other written teaching.

Who could keep up with it all? Would not papal teaching receive more attention, be more closely studied and assimilated, if there were rather less of it? It is sometimes said that it will take a century for the Church to absorb the body of teaching by John Paul II, but that is unrealistic. A century from now, another pope will be teaching the Church and will expect, quite reasonably, that people heed what *he* says. Leaving aside scholars and graduate students, who among us now reads Pope Leo XIII's eighty-six encyclicals, with the sole exception of the landmark 1891 social encyclical *Rerum Novarum*? Who would have time to do that and also keep up with the output by the present pope and his immediate predecessors?

As the stream of papal teaching has grown to a torrent, many diocesan bishops seem to have had less to say. This has not been a healthy development for them or their churches. Vatican II says in *Lumen Gentium*: "Among the more important duties of bishops that of preaching the Gospel has pride of place. . . . They are authentic teachers, that is, teachers endowed with the authority of Christ, who preach the faith to the people assigned to them." They need to bear witness in their own voices to the truths of faith and morals, lest Catholic teaching come to be regarded as merely the pope's slant on things.

But bishops have not surrendered the work of teaching only to the pope. More and more lately, they seem to have been leaving it to their episcopal conferences to speak for them. As we have seen, bishops' conferences do have a teaching role, under conditions spelled out by John Paul II in the 1998 apostolic letter *Apostolos Suos*. But it conflicts with the ecclesiology of *communio* and its emphasis on particular churches for diocesan bishops to cede their teaching responsibilities to episcopal conferences — especially when, in practice, that means ceding them to committees and staff. Yet, in the United States at least, that nevertheless seems to have happened.

This trend should be reversed. Diocesan bishops should regularly teach their people themselves. If they feel inadequate to do that, then, as suggested earlier, the problem should be remedied through study and intellectual formation. Perhaps, too, several bishops of a state or region might now and then issue joint (not collective) pastoral letters in which each would address the people of his own diocese. Something like this already has been done now and then in recent years, and it seems to have had good results.

It is significant that Pope John Paul, discussing bishops' conferences in *Apostolos Suos*, invokes collegiality to pinpoint the intrinsic limitations of these bodies. The bishops of a country or region cannot act collegially just by getting together and doing something, he points out. No doubt the actions of episcopal conferences do have a collegial character of sorts; but only the College of Bishops acts collegially in a full sense — either through an ecumenical council or when the bishops, though dispersed throughout the world, engage in a collegial act recognized as such by the pope. "Equivalent collegial actions cannot be carried out at the level of individual particular Churches or of gatherings of such Churches called together by their respective bishops," he says.

There also is the question of *what* should be taught, whether by popes, episcopal conferences, or diocesan bishops. In recent years, quite a lot of the output at all levels has focused on political and socioeconomic issues. While it sometimes is appropriate that the representatives of the Magisterium speak about such things, that should be done in moderation and only when circumstances make it necessary, lest topics of greater pastoral urgency, closer to the specific competence of the Magisterium, be neglected, and the voice of the laity be silenced in areas where *they* are competent and the responsibility to speak is properly theirs.

Papal travel has been a notable feature of the pontificate of Pope John Paul. These journeys dramatically showcase his extraordinary pastoral charism. Great good has been done in this way, but it may have had a price: the overshadowing of the bishops.

Sometimes bishops badly *want* the pope to come, precisely to give them and the Church locally some much-needed stature and support. This can be the case, for instance, where Catholicism is experiencing political or religious discrimination. Then the pope's appearance on the scene is a useful reminder that local Catholics have a powerful friend and are part of a worldwide communion concerned about their welfare. Elsewhere, as in the secularized countries of the affluent West, the pope can bolster flagging Catholic identity and morale. Fundamentally, too, Petrine ministry is a ministry "from within," not an intervention from without, so that the primate of the universal Church comes to particular churches as a constitutive part of what makes them church; it is an important part of the pope's ministry to affirm and support particular churches and their bishops. "Strengthen your brethren," Jesus told Peter (Luke 22:32).

Nevertheless, if the pope comes too often, people may begin to suppose that the only real authority in the Church is his, while other authority, including the bishops', is derivative or delegated. This impression can be visually reinforced by public events with the pope at center stage, bishops massed behind him or to one side like an opera chorus.

As with papal teaching, the point emphatically is *not* that popes should never travel. Papal visits need rethinking so that they will continue to have as much impact in the future, and do as much good, as up to now. (Note, too, that popes in the future may not choose to travel as much as John Paul simply because they prefer to organize their time differently.)

It seems appropriate, for example, that the pope sometimes attend extraordinary events involving interaction among Church people, especially bishops, at the international level: Eucharistic congresses, meetings of regional bishops' groups, the formal conclusions of Synods, and the like. Now and then, too, popes will want to visit particular countries and regions, take the world stage to deliver important messages at major international secular gatherings (for example, Pope Paul and Pope John Paul at the UN General Assembly), and solemnize major ecumenical or interreligious events. Whenever and however popes travel in the future, the collegial dimension of their visits should be emphasized. And certainly, too, when the pope comes visiting, he should not be put in the position of having to lecture bishops about doing their job.

Synods That Count

The world Synod of Bishops needs big changes. This Vatican II innovation is a necessary part of Church life today; it would be foolish to abolish it, as some angry progressives urge. But it requires a major overhaul.

As matters stand, bishops often enter the deliberations of the Synod inadequately prepared; jet-lagged and overworked, they are rushed through the process without much time to think; they are not allowed to make a substantive collective statement of their own, even their suggestions are supposed to be secret (they rarely are), and it is left to the pope to draw conclusions and publish a final document. Some go home not just tired but indignant.

But the changes should go beyond addressing these matters. If the Synod is to remain purely advisory to the pope, the bishops should at least be permitted to operate freely and give their best answers to specific questions about which the pope actually wants their advice.

While manipulation of the process by the Curia should be ruled out, the problem is a good deal more complicated than critics of the Curia are willing to admit. The impulse of some curial officials to overmanage and overcontrol reflects their not-unfounded fear that, given their heads, some bishops will behave irresponsibly; that is to say, it reflects difficulties with some bishops. Tinkering with Synod rules will not solve that.

Germain Grisez offers the radical suggestion that the pope, after seeking advice from other bishops, turn the Synod into a permanent, representative body that will collaborate with him on matters other than the ministry of unity. But before this step could responsibly be taken, he adds, there would have to be a prior unity in essentials among the world's bishops that, realistically speaking, may not exist today. In other words, the necessary reshaping of the hierarchy comes first.

Supposing episcopal unity to have been restored, however, then — according to Grisez — only by way of exception would the pope make noncollegial use of his supreme authority; supreme teaching and governing authority in the universal Church normally would be exercised collegially — by the pope and the Synod, under the headship of the pope. According to this scheme, the pope would not lose his supreme authority to govern and teach the Church on his own; but he would govern and teach this way only when he deemed it truly necessary.

The Synod would set up offices and structures similar to those of the present Roman Curia. (Lest this simply mean piling new structures on top of old ones, it would be essential to carry out a thoroughgoing reorganization meant to avoid duplication.) The new offices and structures, together with the Synod members' own relationships with other bishops and regional church structures, would largely replace nuncios and apostolic delegates. The pope would continue to have advisers and assistants to help him in matters he reserved to himself as well as in his role as head of the Synod and in his dealings with bishops' conferences, local churches, and others with whom he chose to deal directly.

Under this plan, the national conferences would not become more important but rather less; the more important regional structures would be groupings of archdioceses, which would elect members to the Synod. Probably, too, there would be less need for ecumenical councils — and certainly none for a council every ten or twenty-five years — since communications technology would make it possible for decision-makers in Rome to consult the world's bishops regularly, frequently, and directly, and get their consent whenever doing so seemed appropriate.

As noted, a proposal like this takes for granted the prior existence of an ideal state of affairs: a degree of harmony on essentials among bishops and between bishops and the pope that may not now exist. It also involves a number of untested imponderables. Yet it does recognize the respective claims of papal primacy and episcopal collegiality, and goes much further in attempting to balance and integrate them than anything else on the table up to now. This specific plan may not now be feasible and may never be. There is no doubt, however, that a better working relationship between primacy and collegiality is needed. So, therefore, are creative and responsible suggestions for bringing it about.

Back to the Future?

"In the first millennium," remarks Cardinal Danneels, "the exercise of primacy was completely different from the way it was conceived of and lived in the second millennium. I don't think we can exclude that in the third millennium we may find a different form of application."

For obvious ecumenical reasons, centering especially on the hope for Orthodox-Catholic reunion, it often is said that the first millennium should be the model in reshaping the exercise of papal primacy and the relationship of Rome to local churches. Pope John Paul puts it like this in *Ut Unum Sint*:

> The Church's journey began in Jerusalem on the day of Pentecost and its original expansion in the *oikoumene* [civilized world] of that time was centered around Peter and the Eleven (cf. Acts 2.14). The structures of the Church in the East and in the West evolved in reference to that apostolic heritage. Her unity during the first millennium was maintained within those same structures through the Bishops, Successors of the Apostles, in communion with the Bishop of Rome. If today at the end of the second millennium we are seeking to restore full communion, it is to that unity, thus structured, which we must look.

Hermann Pottmeyer says particular attention should go to "the understanding, form, and practice of the Petrine office in the first centuries when the church was still undivided and understood itself to be an ecumenical community of churches." Although ecclesial communion was repeatedly ruptured in the first millennium by heresy and schism, nevertheless it was generally recognized that communion was the state willed by Christ for the universal Church; when divisions occurred, all, or nearly all, agreed that they should be repaired.

As for the papacy in those first thousand years, Vatican Council II had this to say in its Decree on Ecumenism, *Unitatis Redintegratio*:

> For many centuries the Churches of the East and of the West went their own ways, though a brotherly com-

munion of faith and sacramental life bound them together. If disagreements in faith and discipline arose among them, the Roman See acted by common consent as moderator.

This moderating role appears to have consisted largely of identifying the norm of apostolicity in faith and, in case of disputes, determining whether (and which) contesting local churches and Christians were living up to it.

One can hardly quarrel with the intention of the council and the pope, eager to promote reunion of East and West, in stressing the positive, while leaving some less than positive facts unmentioned. If we are now to move closer to unity, though, it becomes all the more imperative to be realistic about these less than positive realities, even at the risk of causing embarrassment to one side or the other, or both.

One unpleasant contemporary fact of religious life is the persistence of Orthodox-Catholic tensions. In the Orthodox-Roman Catholic dialogue of the last thirty years, Rome often has sounded a great deal more eager for reunion than its Orthodox interlocutors. The leaders of the Russian Orthodox and Greek Orthodox Churches have taken an especially hard line, while the present Ecumenical Patriarch of Constantinople has said things suggesting that reunion of East and West is an eschatological ideal — something not to be realized until the end of time. This is hardly encouraging.

Certain realities about the first millennium also need to be recognized. One is that, even if the understanding of papal primacy then had been more developed than it actually was, sociological circumstances, including the difficulty of travel and communication, would have ruled out the exercise of primacy in anything like its present form. Geographical isolation and poor communications undoubtedly impeded growth in understanding of the doctrine. The practice of the first millennium therefore cannot be taken as normative and definitive in some simplistic way.

The domination of the Eastern Church by the emperor in Constantinople, as well as the emperor's efforts — sometimes all too successful — to dominate the Bishop of Rome, also must be taken into account in trying to understand the exercise of papal primacy in the first millennium. At a time when popes had their hands full trying — not always successfully — to fend off imperial control, loud and frequent papal claims to exercise primacy over the emperor's court church in Constantinople were hardly to be expected.

In sum, we should not take a naïve and ahistorical view of an exceedingly complex, and often troubled, period in Church events. That is not to say there is nothing there to help the search for a new way of exercising papal primacy. "Attempts in the past had their limits, deriving from the mentality of the times and the very understanding of the truths about the Church," John Paul wrote in his 1995 apostolic letter on the Eastern Church, *Orientale Lumen.* But "today we know that unity can be achieved through the love of God only if the Churches want it together, in full respect for the traditions of each and for necessary autonomy"; it will not come about by "claiming that the whole array of uses and customs in the Latin Church is more complete or better suited to showing the fullness of correct doctrine."

Part of the change in thinking and practice will no doubt require respecting the traditional system of polity in the Eastern Churches, including the role of patriarchs and synodal structures of decision-making, not in place of, but alongside, the universal primacy of the pope. Finding a system that is mutually agreeable and faithful to the constitution of the Church will be difficult, to say the least.

Among other things, it may mean taking a closer look at the pope's role as Western Patriarch, and distinguishing this from what he does as universal pastor and as Bishop of Rome. The tendency for a long time has been to conflate the three roles. Separating out functions proper to each, without doing violence to primacy, will be an extremely sensitive task requiring honest scholarship and careful discernment by the Magisterium.

Another area for exploration concerns the synodal form of decision-making in the Church. Today, when Catholics use the word "synod," they commonly mean the assemblies of the world Synod of Bishops. But "synod" also refers to much else. In fact, a synodal system would involve a network of councils at various levels — diocesan, regional, national, international — through which bishops, priests, religious, and laypeople could participate in decision-making.

Tertullian spoke of synods as early as the fourth century, and for a long time such gatherings were held frequently. Synods played an important role in the renewal of the Church after the sixteenth-century Council of Trent. But they fell out of favor as part of the reaction against Conciliarism, especially after the so-called Council of Pistoia in 1786 issued decrees (which Pius VI condemned) claiming that synods had independent authority. The 1917 Code of Canon Law tried without much success to revive the idea. The 1983 Code contains a number of canons on the diocesan synod — defined as "a group of selected priests and other Christian faithful of a particular church which offers assistance to the diocesan bishop" (canon 460) — and specifies that such a gathering be held whenever the diocesan bishop considers it warranted (canon 461). A number of dioceses around the world have had synods in recent years.

Provincial and national synods also are part of the picture. Speaking in June, 1999, at the close of the Second Plenary Synod of Poland, Pope John Paul briefly reviewed the history of synods, and concluded that through them "successive generations sought for themselves new ways of living the Christian life" and made "a precious contribution to the development and activity of the Church." As archbishop of Cracow, Cardinal Karol Wojtyla organized a notable diocesan synod after Vatican Council II.

Opening up the decision-making process can involve problems. One is the risk that synods or other bodies might fall into the hands of liberal activists, Church bureaucrats, and special interest groups. That appears to be what happened in the case of the Dutch National Pastoral Council after Vatican II and is what quite clearly happened at the U.S. Call To Action Conference, held in Detroit in 1976 as part of the bishops' observance of the American bicentennial. Although Call To Action was not itself a synod, disgust with Call To Action led to the shelving of the synodal model thereafter.

Still, the idea of regular mixed assemblies of the faithful as an element in decision-making *could* be revived, provided safeguards were adopted to avoid earlier mistakes. Procedures would be required to ensure that participants were truly representative of active, mature, and faithful clergy, religious, and laity, and that bishops retained the right to decide what topics would be treated. The tendency to cater to dissidents — often visible in Church circles in recent years — would have to be resisted. The distinction between deliberation and decision-making would have to be understood and maintained, including the idea that although everyone should get a reasonable hearing, not everyone should vote; and bishops would retain the prerogative of accepting or rejecting the acts of any synod. If these things were done, a system of synods could emerge as part of an effort to reach agreement with the Orthodox and other Christian bodies in which these bodies play an important role.

Among these are the Anglicans; and it should be recalled that the Anglican-Roman Catholic statement "The Gift of Authority" expresses enthusiasm for "a universal primacy, exercised collegially in the context of synodality." Among the areas of Anglican-Catholic progress noted in the document is "synodality and its implications for the communion of the whole people of God and of all the local churches." The statement points out:

> The Roman Catholic Church, especially since the Second Vatican Council, has been gradually developing synodal structures for sustaining *koinonia* [community] more effectively. The developing role of national and regional Episcopal Conferences and the regular holding of General Assemblies of the Synod of Bishops demonstrate this evolution. There has also been renewal in the exercise of synodality at the local level, although this varies from place to place. Canonical legislation now requires lay men and women, persons in the religious life, deacons and priests to play a part in parochial and diocesan pastoral councils, diocesan synods and a variety of other bodies, whenever these are convened.

The idea is worth exploring. Still, it is important to bear in mind that the Catholic Church cannot reasonably be expected to buy into the Anglican system of local autonomy, as described by the then-archbishop of Canterbury, Robert Runcie, in a letter to John Paul II in 1988. Pope John Paul had written him about the problem raised for Catholic-Anglican relations by the priestly ordination of women in "some provinces of the Anglican communion." Archbishop Runcie replied that neither he as archbishop of Canterbury nor the Lambeth Conference, the highest-level Anglican structure of governance, had "juridical authority over the Anglican Communion"; rather, Anglican provinces have "the canonical authority to implement the mission of the Church as they deem right in their own cultures."

No doubt that arrangement would be congenial to some of today's Roman Catholic advocates of devolution; but it illustrates why the Catholic Church, committed to unity grounded in a shared understanding of ecclesial common good and what pertains to it, cannot simply adopt an Anglican or Orthodox system of decision-making. That nevertheless leaves room to experiment with some version of synodality as a basis for ecumenical discussions with the Anglicans and the Orthodox. (It might also have the attractive result of offering an alternative to the continued expansion of the "photocopying Church" — von Balthasar's name for ecclesiastical bureaucracy — that has become a problematical feature of Catholic life since Vatican Council II.)

The distinguished Anglican theologian John Macquarrie suggests an approach to papal primacy according to which "papal jurisdiction might be exercised in different ways in different parts of the Church, according to local circumstances."

> Thus, within the diocese of Rome, it is obvious that the jurisdiction of the Pope would be immediate and direct. Within the Church in Italy, it would be somewhat less direct, because the Pope would be in collegial relationship with the Italian primates, such as the Patriarch of Venice. In the case of the Church in France, let us say, or Germany or the United States, the mode of jurisdiction would be modified further. When we come to an entity like the Church of England or the whole world-

wide Anglican communion, my suggestion [is] that papal jurisdiction should be exercised through the existing primates, namely the Archbishops of Canterbury, York and the other primatial sees.

Something along these lines might be worth exploring in some circumstances. But, as Dr. Macquarrie makes clear, his suggestion would involve a "delegation of authority" by the pope to the Anglican primates; and if, as Archbishop Runcie told John Paul II in 1988, Anglican primates do not have "juridical authority over the Anglican communion," it is hard to see what good it would do for Rome to delegate to Anglican primates authority they could not exercise and the faithful under their jurisdiction would not respond to.

The lesson may simply be that, as necessary as changes in the structures of papal primacy very likely are for ecumenism's sake, much more than structural change will be needed to achieve Christian unity. Roman Catholics are not the only ones who will have to change.

In the End, Primacy

The ways in which papal primacy and episcopal collegiality are exercised will always be open to improvement. Today, this question must be considered in light of John Paul II's dramatic invitation to new thinking about papal primacy as it relates to the quest for Christian unity. In February, 2000, during one of his pilgrimages, he repeated his appeal in an address during an ecumenical service in the Coptic Catholic cathedral in Cairo. "My dear brothers, there is not time to lose," he exclaimed to an audience representing all of Egypt's major Christian groups.

Even in the face of this urgency, however, it is necessary to recognize that a number of proposals for taming the pope fall short of what is required, either from a doctrinal point of view or from the perspective of good sense. Some — like holding ecumenical councils on a regular basis every ten or twenty-five years, or having bishops chosen locally and merely confirmed by the pope — do not, strictly speaking, conflict with any doctrine of faith but would seriously weaken the papacy and ecclesial communion.

As we have seen, problems arise when the Church is understood in sociopolitical terms that ignore the fundamental fact that its common good — divine-human communion — is a gift of God to be faithfully preserved, not a goal to be achieved by human effort; when the principle of subsidiarity or any other rationale for local autonomy is pushed so far that local churches are set in opposition to the universal Church or congregationalism is encouraged; when a parochial version of inculturation is treated as if it were a value superior to integral Catholic identity and unity in the truth. There is something to be said for democracy, subsidiarity, inculturation, and pluralism in the Church, but not at the expense of ecclesial communion.

The nineteenth-century British historian Thomas Babington Macaulay was no friend of Catholicism. Writing in the manner of an honest British bigot of his day, he observed of the "polity of the Church of Rome" that "among the contrivances which have been devised for deceiving and oppressing mankind, it occupies the highest place." Still, looking at Rome from a human point of view, Macaulay couldn't help but be impressed.

In the century before his own, he wrote, the Church's influence was "constantly on the decline," while the papacy itself was "brought so low as to be an object of derision to infidels, and of pity rather than of hatred to Protestants." Think of Pius VI — "Citizen Braschi, exercising the profession of Pontiff" — dying in the clutches of Revolutionary France.

But the end was not yet. . . . Even before the funeral rites had been performed over the ashes of Pius the Sixth a great reaction had commenced, which . . . appears to be still in progress. Anarchy had had its day. A new order of things rose out of the confusion, new dynasties, new laws, new titles; and amidst them emerged the ancient religion. The Arabs have a fable that the Great Pyramid was built by antediluvian kings, and alone, of all the works of men, bore the weight of the flood. Such as this was the fate of the Papacy. It had been buried under the great inundation; but its deep foundations had remained unshaken; and when the waters abated, it appeared alone amidst the ruins of a world which had passed away.

That was 1840. The phenomenon had been repeated many times before Macaulay's day. It is likely to be repeated many times in the future.

There is something more than merely prudent human calculation in the Catholic focus on Rome. One sees at work something of the insight voiced by St. Ignatius of Antioch, who saluted Roman Christians in luminous terms as, early in the second century, he made his way to martyrdom in their city.

Ignatius, who is also called Theophorus, to the Church which has found mercy, through the majesty of the Most High Father, and Jesus Christ, His only-begotten Son; the Church that is beloved and enlightened . . . the Church that presides in the capital of the Romans, worthy of God, worthy of honor, worthy of the highest happiness, worthy of praise, worthy of obtaining her every desire, worthy of being deemed holy, the Church that presides in love.

Earlier I promised not to quote Scripture for the sake of apologetics. But I cannot bring this modest study to a close without quoting Galatians 2:11-14. St. Paul writes:

> But when Cephas [Peter] came to Antioch I opposed him to his face, because he stood condemned. For before certain men came from James, he ate with the Gentiles; but when they came he drew back and separated himself, fearing the circumcision party. And with him the rest of the Jews acted insincerely, so that even Barnabas was carried away by their insincerity. But when I saw they were not straightforward about the truth of the gospel, I said to Cephas before them all, "If you, though a Jew, live like a Gentile and not like a Jew, how can you compel the Gentiles to live like Jews?"

This is hardly a proof text for primacy. Paul writes against the background of his long conflict with the Judaizers — Jewish Christians who maintained that Gentiles converting to Christianity should be circumcised and required to observe the dietary laws and other customs of the old religion. This was something the man from Tarsus violently opposed, for it called into question the efficacy of the redemption won by Christ.

Paul believed he had Peter (Cephas) on his side. Earlier in his career, he had made it a point to visit Peter in Jerusalem, in recognition of his authority (cf. Galatians 1:18). But, in the episode described here, Peter has turned fickle. Visiting Antioch, an important Christian center in the early days, he freely associated with Gentile converts and shared meals with them; but when Judaizers from Jerusalem criticized him, Peter and other Jewish converts withdrew from the Gentiles' company. Paul was furious. And he reports that, in the incident narrated here, he "opposed [Peter] to his face" for backsliding.

Peter wavers, and Paul takes him to task. At first this does not look a lot like primacy.

Look closer. Paul's pride about the chutzpah he showed in opposing Peter makes sense only on the supposition that Paul and everyone else in the apostolic Church recognized Peter's position of unique authority. Paul does not boast of having corrected Judaizers or James or Barnabas; he boasts about having given Cephas a piece of his mind because Cephas is the human Rock on whom Christ founded his Church.

Catholics believe the same position as rocklike guarantor of faith and unity has been occupied in the Church for two thousand years by Peter's successors, the Bishops of Rome, and will continue to be occupied by them as long as Christianity lasts. To put that simply: Catholics believe in the primacy of the pope.

How the Pope Is Elected

No doubt about it, the white smoke is a thrill. Late in the day on October 16, 1978, I was marking time with a bunch of reporters in the Sala Stampa della Santa Sede — the Vatican press office — when there it was on the TV screen: a wisp, a puff, a steady stream, billowing from the gimcrack chimney on the Sistine Chapel roof. Having been fooled before, we watched intently. Yes, no . . . definitely yes.

"It's white!" Someone let out a whoop, and we burst from the Sala Stampa into St. Peter's Square. The crowd was gathering. A short time later Karol Wojtyla was presented to us as Pope John Paul II. Standing in the loggia above the basilica's entrance, he cried out, "Praised be Jesus Christ!" "Now and forever," the people replied. The rest, as they say, is history.

Now John Paul's visible frailty is a poignant reminder that the Church and the world will be watching for the white smoke again one of these days — please God, not too soon. The stakes in the next papal election will be very high.

Among the questions facing the cardinals will be these: Is the Church ready for a Third World pope? Do we need another ecumenical council just now? How should tensions between the claims of episcopal collegiality and papal primacy be worked out? What concessions, if any, should be offered the Orthodox (possibly others, too) for unity's sake? Should John Paul's embrace of the "new movements" in the Church and his strong stands on things like women priests and clerical celibacy, contraception and abortion, and sacraments for the divorced and remarried, be maintained — or should they be downplayed, even quietly shelved?

Whenever the next conclave does take place, understanding it will require understanding the process. In the early centuries of the Church the Bishop of Rome was chosen by the clergy and people of the city, but since 1179 the cardinals have been the only electors. The sole exception was in 1417, when thirty representatives of the Council of Constance helped elect Cardinal Odo Colonna as Pope Martin V, thereby ending the Great Schism of the West.

The cardinals choose the pope in a gathering called a conclave. The word means "with a key," recalling the days when electors were locked up, sometimes for months, until the job was done. Although nowadays the conclave is held in the Sistine Chapel, attached to the Apostolic Palace, there have been many conclaves outside Rome — the last was in 1800 — and, during the nineteenth and twentieth centuries, a few in Rome but outside the Sistine.

Many popes have set rules for the conclave. The basic pattern was established by Pope Alexander III in 1179, with changes and refinements added in the century just past by Pope St. Pius X, Pope Pius XI, Pope Pius XII, Pope John XXIII, and Pope Paul VI. In *Romano Pontifici Eligendo*, published in 1975, Paul VI set the top number of cardinal-electors at one hundred twenty and decreed that cardinals aged eighty and above may not vote.

The latest legislation, which will be controlling at the next conclave, is contained in the apostolic constitution *Universi Dominici Gregis* ("the Lord's whole flock"), published by Pope John Paul in 1996. Close familiarity with this detailed, somewhat repetitious document will be indispensable to anyone who wants to know what's going on.

It begins by reaffirming that the cardinals, no one else, are the papal electors. Two reasons are given: because of their traditional link with the Bishop of Rome (cardinals were originally senior clergy of the Roman Church) and because the cardinals, coming from every continent, express the Church's universality and the universal outreach of Petrine ministry. The apostolic constitution also confirms Pope Paul's rules that cardinal-electors shall number no more than one hundred twenty and that cardinals eighty and older may not vote. (At the end of 1999, there were one hundred six, out of a total of one hundred fifty-four.)

Universi Dominici Gregis goes into considerable detail about the interregnum, the time between the old pope's death and the conclave. Besides performing ritual duties, the College of Cardinals — including those eighty and over — is to assemble daily in a "general congregation" presided over by its Dean, currently the Benin-born Cardinal Bernardin Gantin, former prefect of the curial Congregation for Bishops. Here the cardinals are to conduct the necessary business of the Church (but not do things like naming bishops that are reserved to the pope) and prepare for the conclave. Routine matters are handled by "particular congregations" consisting of the Camerlengo (chamberlain) of the Holy Roman Church, at present the Spanish Cardinal Eduardo Martinez Somalo, prefect of the Congregation for Institutes of Consecrated Life and Societies of Apostolic Life, and three cardinal-assistants.

What the cardinals really do at these daily gatherings, of course, is take one another's measure. True, they've been doing that for years at consistories, synods, assemblies of Roman congregations, and other events, as well as in one-on-one encounters. But now, with a papal election imminent, the question is acute: Which one of us shall it be?

Universi Dominici Gregis forbids electioneering and deal-making. "The cardinal electors shall abstain from any form of pact, agreement, promise or other commitment of any kind. . . . [They are] not to allow themselves to be guided . . . by friendship or aversion, or to be influenced by favor or personal relationships towards anyone, or to be constrained by the interference of persons in authority or by pressure groups, by the suggestions of the mass media, or by force, fear or the pursuit of popularity." Instead, they should vote for the person (not necessarily a cardinal, though almost certainly the next pope will come from their ranks) whom they judge "most suited to govern the universal Church in a fruitful and beneficial way."

But John Paul strikes this realistic note: "It is not my intention . . . to forbid, during the period in which the See is vacant, the exchange of views concerning the election." Views will be exchanged, in the general congregations and in other more private settings.

Depending on how long it takes the electors to get to Rome (no problem in this age of jets, though in earlier times cardinals coming from afar sometimes missed the voting), the conclave will begin at least fifteen and no more than twenty days after the pope's death. Formerly, the cardinals were obliged to rough it in cramped, temporary cubicles in the Apostolic Palace, but next time they will be in the Domus Sanctae Marthae — St. Martha's House — a new twenty-million-dollar hotellike residence behind the Vatican Audience Hall. While not luxurious, its air-conditioned two-room suites with private baths are comfortable by any standards.

The cardinals start the conclave's first day by celebrating Mass together in St. Peter's, then go in solemn procession to the Sistine. There the Dean of the College reads out an oath to which each must individually subscribe:

"We . . . promise, pledge, and swear that whichever of us by divine disposition is elected Roman Pontiff will commit himself faithfully to carrying out the *munus Petrinum* [Petrine office] of Pastor of the Universal Church and will not fail to affirm and defend strenuously the spiritual and temporal rights of the Holy See.

"In a particular way, we promise and swear to observe with the greatest fidelity and with all persons, clerical or lay, secrecy regarding everything that in any way relates to the election of the Roman Pontiff and regarding what occurs in the place of the election, directly or indirectly related to the results of the voting . . . and never to lend support or favor to any interference, opposition or any other form of intervention, whereby secular authorities of whatever order or degree or any group of people or individuals might wish to intervene."

The theme of secrecy runs throughout the apostolic constitution. Security specialists are to check the Sistine for bugs. The cardinals are not to communicate with anyone outside. Newspapers, radio, and TV are banned (the Internet isn't mentioned, but its banning can be presumed). If the electors keep vote tallies, these are to be collected after each ballot and burned. The handful of staff allowed to be present (the secretary of the College of Cardinals, three masters of ceremonies, two sacristans, a clerical assistant to the Dean, two physicians) are under equally tight wraps.

Whether or not one considers this concern for secrecy excessive depends on one's estimate of the chances of history repeating itself. Obviously John Paul's intention is to forestall outside interference; and it is a fact that emperors, kings, and even angry mobs often have interfered in papal elections. As recently as the conclave of 1903, the Austrian Emperor Franz Joseph, exercising the right of veto often used by Catholic rulers over the centuries, turned thumbs-down on Cardinal Mariano Rampolla, Leo XIII's Secretary of State. Word of the veto was brought to the conclave by the cardinal-archbishop of

Cracow, a performance *Universi Dominici Gregis* forbids any cardinal to repeat.

With the preliminaries completed, the election begins.

In principle, there formerly were three methods for choosing a pope: acclamation, according to which, *quasi inspiratione* — as if by inspiration — the cardinals spontaneously recognized someone as Supreme Pontiff; *per compromissum*, in which authority to make the choice was delegated to a small group; and secret ballot by the body as a whole. Pope John Paul eliminates acclamation and delegation, seldom or never used in any case, and retains only the third method — *per scrutinium*, or "scrutiny."

On the first day there is to be, at most, only one ballot, in the afternoon, but thereafter there are four ballots daily — two in the morning, two in the afternoon. Each cardinal writes the name of his choice ("in handwriting that cannot be identified as his") on a rectangular piece of paper with the words *Eligo in Summum Pontificem* ("I choose as Supreme Pontiff") at the top. The paper is folded twice and placed in a receptacle at the altar, while the elector says aloud, "I call as my witness Christ the Lord who will be my judge, that my vote is given to the one who before God I think should be elected." The apostolic constitution also provides for collecting ballots from sick cardinals back in the Domus Sanctae Marthae. The votes are counted by three cardinal-"scrutineers," with the name on each ballot read out to the electors at the end of the count. After the counting the ballots are burned, producing the famous smoke. (Chemicals are used to make it black or white.)

If no one has been chosen after three days, there is a pause of up to one day for prayer, "informal discussion among the voters," and a brief spiritual exhortation by the senior cardinal-deacon. At this point, the so-called "great electors" — cardinals good at negotiating agreements and organizing voting blocs

— become especially important. Had they lived, Cardinal Joseph Bernardin of Chicago and Cardinal Basil Hume, O.S.B., of Westminster would have been great electors; Cardinal Godfried Danneels of Mechelen-Brussels, Belgium, may be one next time.

After the pause, voting continues for another seven ballots, followed by another pause, seven more ballots, and so on, until there have been up to thirty-four ballots extending over ten or twelve days. At this point, *Universi Dominici Gregis* introduces its most striking innovation.

Up to now, following long tradition, election has required two-thirds of the votes (or, if the total number of electors is not divisible into three equal parts, two-thirds plus one — seventy-one votes in the voting body of one hundred six as it stood at the end of 1999). But, this point in the conclave having been reached, the Camerlengo is to invite the cardinals to "express an opinion about the manner of proceeding" — and the election will then go forward as the majority decides. Even so, the requirement of a majority vote cannot be waived; one way to get a majority quickly, the apostolic constitution points out, is to vote on the two candidates who got the most votes in the previous round.

John Paul does not explain his reasons for this change, but sparing the Church the ordeal of a drawn-out papal election, such as many in the past have been, must surely have been one. There are different views of the practical results.

Thomas Reese, S.J., says that under the old two-thirds rule, cardinals had to "compromise and look for a consensus candidate." Now a determined majority far short of two-thirds need only dig in, knowing it will prevail in the end; hence "the likelihood of a more radical and ideological candidate being elected pope." That could be. But it is important to bear in mind that this electoral body craves consensus. If, after a week and a half of balloting, members of a slim majority saw no chance of generating more support for their man, rather than ram him through when the rules changed, they might be moved to join their brothers in the minority in finding a candidate nearly all could accept. The electors' mood at the time will be crucial, and no one can know that in advance.

Once a man is elected, the Cardinal Dean asks for his consent: "Do you accept your canonical election as Supreme Pontiff?" If he says yes, the Dean asks, "By what name do you wish to be called?" Soon the whole world knows the answer.

Universi Dominici Gregis opens with these words:

"The Shepherd of the Lord's whole flock is the Bishop of the Church of Rome, where the Blessed Apostle Peter, by sovereign disposition of divine Providence, offered to Christ the supreme witness of martyrdom by the shedding of his blood. It is therefore understandable that the lawful apostolic succession in this See . . . has always been the object of particular attention."

Understandable indeed. As we shall all be reminded again one of these days.

Sources

Official sources such as papal encyclicals, council documents, and documents from dicasteries of the Holy See are identified in the text. Other sources consulted in writing this book include the following.

Association for the Rights of Catholics in the Church, *A Proposed Constitution of the Catholic Church*, We-Are-Church website, 1999; Hans Urs von Balthasar, *The Office of Peter and the Structure of the Church* (San Francisco: Ignatius Press, 1986); Umberto Benigni, "Ultramontanism," *The Catholic Encyclopedia*; Leonardo Boff, *Church: Charism & Power: Liberation Theology and the Institutional Church* (New York: The Crossroad Publishing Company, 1985); Michael J. Buckley, S.J., *Papal Primacy and the Episcopate: Towards a Relational Understanding* (New York: The Crossroad Publishing Company, 1998); Matthew Bunson, *Our Sunday Visitor's Encyclopedia of Catholic History* (Huntington, Ind.: Our Sunday Visitor Publishing Division, 1995).

Paul Collins, "Stress on Papal Primacy Led to Exaggerated Clout for a Pope Among Equals," *National Catholic Reporter*, October 24, 1997; John Cornwell, *Hitler's Pope: The Secret History of Pius XII* (New York: Viking, 1999); Cardinal Godfried Danneels, "On Papal Primacy and Decentralization," *Origins*, October 20, 1997; St. Francis de Sales, *The Catholic Controversy* (Rockford, Ill.: Tan Books and Publishers, 1989); Audrey Donnithorne, "China's Drowned Churches," *The Tablet*, September 18, 1999; Eamon Duffy, *Saints and Sinners: A History of the Popes* (New Haven: Yale University Press, 1997); Avery Dulles, S.J., *Models of the Church* (New York: Doubleday Image Books, 1978), and review of Zagano and Tilley, *The Exercise of the Primacy*, Buckley, *Papal Primacy*, and

Pottmeyer, *Towards a Papacy in Communion*, *The Thomist*, April, 1999.

Adrian Fortescue, *The Early Papacy to the Synod of Chalcedon in 451* (Southampton: The Saint Austin Press, 1997); Cardinal Francis George, "How Globalization Challenges the Church's Mission," *Origins*, December 16, 1999; Asterios Gerostergios, *Justinian the Great: The Emperor and Saint* (Belmont, Mass.: Institute for Byzantine and Modern Greek Studies, 1982); Patrick Granfield, O.S.B., "The Concept of the Church as Communion," *Origins*, April 22, 1999; Germain Grisez, *The Way of the Lord Jesus Volume Four: Clerical and Consecrated Life and Service. Tentative Outline — Plan of Research* (privately printed and circulated, 1998); Bernard Häring, "Church Needs Renewed Petrine Ministry," *National Catholic Reporter*, October 17, 1997; William Henn, O.F.M. Cap., "Historical-Theological Synthesis of the Relation Between Primacy and Episcopacy During the Second Millennium" in *Il Primato del Successore di Pietro: Atti del simposio teologico, Roma, dicembre 1996* (Vatican City: Libreria Editrice Vaticana, 1998); Philip Hughes, *A History of the Church* (London: Sheed and Ward, 1979), and *A Popular History of the Catholic Church* (New York: Doubleday Image Books, 1954).

J.N.D. Kelly, *The Oxford Dictionary of Popes* (Oxford: Oxford University Press, 1986); Geoffrey Kirk, "My Wounded Church," *The Tablet*, July 31, 1999; J. P. Kirsch, "The Reformation," *The Catholic Encyclopedia*; Joseph Komonchak, "Ecclesiology of Vatican II," *Origins*, April 22, 1999; Cardinal Franz König, "My Vision for the Church of the Future," *The Tablet*, March 27, 1999; Hans Küng, *Infallible? An Unresolved Enquiry* (New York: Continuum Publishing Company, 1994); Friedrich Lauchert, "Febronianism," *The Catholic Encyclopedia*; J. F. Louglin, "Congregationalism," *The Catholic Encyclopedia*; Thomas Babington Macaulay, "Ranke's History of the Popes" in *Critical and Historical Essays*, volume two (London: J. M. Dent & Sons, Everyman's Library, 1951); John Macquarrie, "The Papacy in a Unified Church," *Pacifica* 2 (1989); Richard P. McBrien, *The Remaking of the Church: An Agenda for Reform* (New York: Harper & Row, 1973); J. Michael Miller, C.S.B., *The Shepherd and the Rock: Origins, Development, and Mission of the Papacy* (Huntington, Ind.: Our Sunday Visitor Publishing Division, 1995).

John Henry Newman, *An Essay on the Development of Christian Doctrine* (New York: Doubleday Image Books, 1960); Terence L. Nichols, *That All May Be One: Hierarchy and Participation in the Church* (Collegeville, Minn.: The Liturgical Press, 1997); Marvin R. O'Connell, "Not Infallible: Two Histories of the Papacy," *Fellowship of Catholic Scholars Quarterly*, Fall, 1998; Hermann J. Pottmeyer, *Towards a Papacy in Communion: Perspectives from Vatican Councils I and II* (New York: The Crossroad Publishing Company, 1998); Archbishop John R. Quinn, *The Reform of the Papacy: The Costly Call to Christian Unity* (New York: The Crossroad Publishing Company, 1999), and "The Exercise of the Primacy and the Costly Call to Unity" in Phyllis Zagano and Terrence W. Tilley, eds., *The Exercise of the Primacy: Continuing the Dialogue* (New York: The Crossroad Publishing Company, 1998).

Thomas P. Rausch, S.J., "Archbishop Quinn's Task," in Zagano and Tilley, eds., *The Exercise of the Primacy*; Cardinal Joseph Ratzinger, *Church, Ecumenism and Politics: New Essays in Ecclesiology* (New York: The Crossroad Publishing Company, 1988); Thomas J. Reese, S.J., *Inside the Vatican: The Politics and Organization of the Catholic Church* (Cambridge, Mass.: Harvard University Press, 1996); Klaus Schatz, S.J., *Papal Primacy from Its Origins to the Present* (Collegeville, Minn.: The Liturgical Press, 1996); Philip Sherrard, *Church, Papacy, and Schism: A Theological Enquiry* (Limni, Evia,

Greece: Denise Harvey, 1996); Josip Stilinovic, "A Patriot, Not a Nationalist," *Catholic World Report*, August/September, 1998; Francis A. Sullivan, S.J., *Creative Fidelity: Weighing and Interpreting Documents of the Magisterium* (New York: Paulist Press, 1996); Arnold J. Toynbee, *A Study of History* (New York: Dell Publishing Co. Laurel Edition, 1974); Robert Louis Wilken, "Gregory VII and the Politics of the Spirit," *First Things*, January, 1999; Garry Wills, *Papal Sin: Structures of Deceit* (New York: Doubleday, 2000); Ralph M. Wiltgen, S.V.D., *The Rhine Flows into the Tiber: A History of Vatican II* (Devon: Augustine Publishing Company, 1979); Wendy M. Wright, "Searching God's Will Together," in Zagano and Tilley, eds., *The Exercise of the Primacy*.

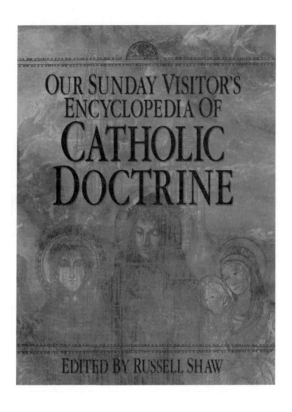

Everything you've ever wanted to know about Catholic
dogma in one convenient volume.
0-87973-**746**-8, hardcover, $39.95, 728 pp.

To order from Our Sunday Visitor:
Toll free: 1-800-348-2440
E-mail: osvbooks@osv.com
Website: www.osv.com

Prices and availability subject to change without notice.

JOHN PAUL II's BOOK OF Mary

COMPILED BY

MARGARET R. BUNSON

The Holy Father has devoted his entire life to Mary. Now
share his profound reflections on our Holy Mother.
0-87973-**578**-3, hardcover, $9.95, 208 pp.

To order from Our Sunday Visitor:
Toll free: 1-800-348-2440
E-mail: osvbooks@osv.com
Website: www.osv.com

Prices and availability subject to change without notice.

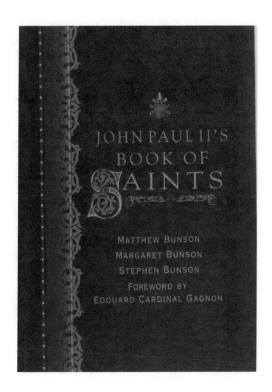

Pope John Paul II has declared these men and women saints
for the entire Church. Here is the most complete list to date.
0-87973-**934**-7, hardcover, $19.95, 384 pp.

To order from Our Sunday Visitor:

Toll free: 1-800-348-2440
E-mail: osvbooks@osv.com
Website: www.osv.com

Prices and availability subject to change without notice.

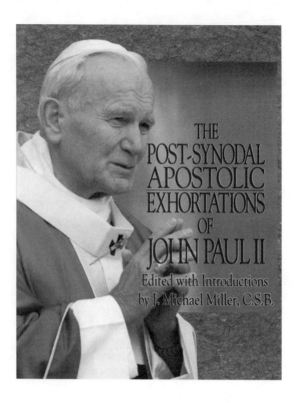

He is truly a man for our season — the thoughts and insights
of the Holy Father on major modern issues.
0-87973-**928**-2, hardcover, $49.95, 800 pp.

To order from Our Sunday Visitor:
Toll free: 1-800-348-2440
E-mail: osvbooks@osv.com
Website: www.osv.com

Our Sunday Visitor. . .
Your Source for Discovering
the Riches of the Catholic Faith

Our Sunday Visitor has an extensive line of materials for young children, teens, and adults. Our books, Bibles, booklets, CD-ROMs, audios, and videos are available in bookstores worldwide.

To receive a FREE full-line catalog or for more information, call **Our Sunday Visitor** at **1-800-348-2440**. Or write, **Our Sunday Visitor** / 200 Noll Plaza / Huntington, IN 46750.

- -

Please send me: ___A catalog
Please send me materials on:

___Apologetics and catechetics   ___Reference works
___Prayer books   ___Heritage and the saints
___The family   ___The parish

Name_____
Address_____Apt._____
City_____State_____Zip_____
Telephone (   ) _____

A09BBABP

- -

Please send a friend: ___A catalog
Please send a friend materials on:

___Apologetics and catechetics   ___Reference works
___Prayer books   ___Heritage and the saints
___The family   ___The parish

Name_____
Address_____Apt._____
City_____State_____Zip_____
Telephone (   ) _____

A09BBABP

- -

Our Sunday Visitor
200 Noll Plaza
Huntington, IN 46750
Toll free: 1-800-348-2440
E-mail: osvbooks@osv.com
Website: www.osv.com